# MEALS
# IN A
# HURRY

# MEALS IN A HURRY

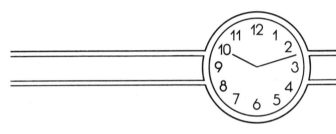

## Speedy Dinners
## for the Busy Cook

### Margaret Happel

**Butterick Publishing**

Art Direction: *Remo Cosentino*
Book Design: *Binnie Weissleder*
Photography: *Gordon E. Smith*

Pictured on the front cover: Shrimp-Chicken Mountain (page 98).

The author and publisher thank the following for supplying props for use in the photography: La Cuisinière, 867 Madison Avenue, New York, NY 10021, Manhattan Ad Hoc Housewares, 842 Lexington Avenue, New York, NY 10021, and Royal Copenhagen Porcelain Company, 573 Madison Avenue, New York, NY 10022.

**Library of Congress Cataloging in Publication Data**

Happel, Margaret.
  Meals in a hurry.

  (A TimeSaver cookbook from Butterick)
  Includes index.
  1. Cookery.  I. Title.  II. Series:  TimeSaver
cookbook from Butterick.
TX715.H254      641.5'55      79-26105
ISBN 0-88421-048-0

# CONTENTS

Introduction                                    7

1  Thirty-Minute Main Courses                   9

2  Forty-Five Minute Main Courses              31

3  Sixty-Minute Menus                          59

4  Five Cook-Ahead Days                        99

Index                                          134

# Introduction

*S*hort on time? MEALS IN A HURRY lets you beat the clock with several effective techniques for producing tasty, home-cooked meals fast.

Make a main dish in 30 minutes and you have the heart of a great meal. The first chapter shows how with shortcuts, quick cooking methods and the use of top-quality convenience foods. With these main dishes you'll have the basis for family lunches, suppers and dinners.

Can you eke out another 15 minutes? In just 45 minutes you can have a more substantial, more sophisticated entrée. Turn to the second chapter for these fast and flavorful main dishes.

When company's coming, look to the chapter on 60-minute menus. Here you'll find over 20 gourmet meals to choose from. Simply follow the work plan and you'll be ready to sit down to a full-course feast in an hour or less.

Would you like to serve a down-home, old-fashioned and totally fussless meal—in minutes? The final chapter has the solution. By devoting a day to cooking you can efficiently make a wide variety of dishes that can be stored until needed. You'll find detailed charts to guide you through the five cook-ahead days, including directions for freezing and reheating.

The next time you're wondering what in the world to concoct for tonight's dinner, make those minutes count with any of the recipes in this book. Then sit back and enjoy the meal—and the compliments.

Note: Throughout MEALS IN A HURRY, oven preheating is necessary only when called for in a recipe. Baking times have been adjusted accordingly.

# THIRTY-MINUTE MAIN COURSES

## CHAPTER ONE

**T**ime is priceless. With the busy schedules so many people keep, finding the time to eat well is often difficult. There's no longer any excuse not to, though, for here is an assortment of hearty main dishes that can be prepared from start to finish in 30 minutes or less. All that is needed to round out the meal is a tossed salad and some warm bread.

To be able to step into the kitchen and prepare many of these meals instantly, try to keep these staples stashed in your cupboard, refrigerator or freezer:

- Canned soups, meats, pork and beans, and the like. Combined with other ingredients, these can form the basis for tasty meals in just moments.
- Dairy foods, such as milk, cream, eggs, cheese and butter. A nutritious meal, perhaps Rarebit on Toast, will never be more than minutes away.
- Canned and frozen vegetables, and fresh vegetables that store well such as onions and celery. They can turn the simplest dish into a filling main course.
- Herbs, spices, sauces, salad dressings and relishes. Choose from the very best quality to add flavor to your dish.
- Unusual convenience foods. Look for vacuum-packed meats, flavored sausages and canned Chinese-style vegetables to provide interest and variety.
- Whole-grain bread, French bread, refrigerator rolls and biscuit mix. Carefully wrapped breads keep well in the refrigerator or freezer, ready to fill out your meals in a hurry.

The quick and easy main dishes in this chapter bring zest to any meal. Why not try Tangy Chili Con Carne, Veal Champignon or Beef and Bean Orientale tonight?

## THIRTY-MINUTE SAUERBRATEN

3 tablespoons butter or
  margarine
4 beef cube steaks
salt and pepper to taste
one 4-ounce can mushroom
  stems and pieces
3 tablespoons finely
  chopped onion
one ⅞-ounce package
  brown gravy mix
3 tablespoons brown sugar
3 tablespoons cider vinegar
2 gingersnaps, crushed

1.  Melt butter or margarine in a heavy skillet; brown steaks on both sides. Season generously with salt and pepper and remove to a warm platter.

2.  Drain liquid from mushrooms into 1-cup measure. Add water to make 1 cup; set aside. Add mushrooms to skillet; stir in onion. Mix and stir over moderately high heat for 2 or 3 minutes. Add reserved 1 cup liquid; bring to boiling point.

3.  Stir in gravy mix, brown sugar, vinegar and crushed gingersnaps. Bring to boiling point, stirring continuously.

4.  Return steaks to skillet, spooning pan liquid over steaks. Cover and simmer 10 to 15 minutes, until steaks are tender. *Serves 4.*

*Note:* This dish is particularly good with mashed potatoes or potato dumplings made from a mix.

## HAMBURGER STEAK IN WINE SAUCE

1½ pounds lean ground
  beef
1 teaspoon salt
¼ teaspoon pepper
1 tablespoon butter or
  margarine
⅓ cup dry red wine
1 teaspoon lemon juice
½ teaspoon Worcestershire
  sauce
2 teaspoons dried parsley
1 teaspoon instant minced
  onion

1.  In a medium bowl, mix beef, salt and pepper. Shape into 4 patties each about ½ inch thick.

2.  Melt butter or margarine in a skillet over medium-high heat. Add patties and cook for 3 to 7 minutes per side. Remove to warm plates.

3.  Add wine, lemon juice, Worcestershire sauce, parsley and minced onion to the skillet; heat to boiling point. Pour over patties and serve at once. *Serves 4.*

# GUMBO JOES

1½ pounds ground chuck
1 cup chopped onion
one 10¾-ounce can
    condensed chicken
    gumbo soup
½ cup ketchup
2 tablespoons
    Worcestershire sauce
1 teaspoon prepared
    mustard
hamburger buns or English
    muffins

1. Shape ground chuck into 1 or 2 flat patties; cook in a large heavy skillet until well browned on both sides. Break up and crumble patties with a fork; continue to cook until all pink disappears.

2. Push meat to side of skillet. Add onion and sauté 4 or 5 minutes. Remove any excess fat from pan with a baster or kitchen spoon.

3. Add condensed soup, ketchup, Worcestershire sauce and mustard; mix well. Simmer over low heat about 10 minutes, stirring occasionally. Serve on toasted hamburger buns or English muffins. *Serves 4 to 6.*

# BEEF AND BEAN ORIENTALE

1 pound ground chuck
1 cup chopped onion
¼ cup soy sauce
¼ teaspoon garlic powder
¼ teaspoon pepper
one 9-ounce package frozen
    French-style green beans,
    thawed
2 tablespoons butter or
    margarine
2 cups cooked rice
2 eggs, beaten
one 16-ounce can bean
    sprouts, rinsed and
    drained

1. Combine ground chuck and onion in large skillet or wok; stir-fry until meat is browned and onion soft. Leave meat in fairly large chunks.

2. Spoon off any excess fat from skillet; add soy sauce, garlic powder and pepper. Mix well and simmer 2 minutes. Remove from skillet and set aside.

3. Pat thawed green beans dry on paper towels. Heat 1 tablespoon of the butter or margarine in skillet; add green beans. Cook 3 or 4 minutes; stir in the cooked rice. Push rice and beans up to sides of skillet.

4. Melt remaining tablespoon butter or margarine in open center of skillet. Add beaten eggs and stir-fry until just set. Carefully stir rice and bean mixture, then reserved meat mixture, back into eggs.

5. Add rinsed and drained bean sprouts and mix completely but gently. Simmer 1 or 2 minutes until heated through. *Serves 4.*

## TANGY CHILI CON CARNE

1½ pounds ground chuck
1 tablespoon vegetable oil
2 cups finely chopped
  onions
1 tablespoon chili powder
1½ teaspoons salt
½ teaspoon garlic powder
one 32-ounce can tomatoes
one 28-ounce can red
  kidney beans, drained
2 tablespoons sugar
¼ cup cider vinegar

1. Shape ground chuck into 1 or 2 flat patties; cook in a large heavy skillet until well browned on both sides. Break up and crumble patties with a fork; continue to cook until all pink disappears.

2. Pour off all but 2 tablespoons fat from skillet. Add oil and onions; sauté 3 or 4 minutes. Stir in chili powder, salt and garlic powder; cook over moderate heat 5 minutes.

3. Coarsely chop the tomatoes and add them, along with all of the liquid, to the skillet. Add drained beans, sugar and vinegar. Simmer over low heat for 15 to 20 minutes, stirring frequently. *Serves 6 to 8.*

## CHILI-CHEESE CASSEROLE

one 8-ounce package corn
  chips
one 15½-ounce can sloppy
  Joe sandwich sauce
one 15-ounce can chili with
  beans
2 cups grated American or
  Cheddar cheese
½ cup chopped onion
½ cup chopped green
  pepper
1 cup boiling water
8 precooked sausage links

1. Crush corn chips and cover bottom of 2-quart casserole with half.

2. Heat sandwich sauce and chili in medium saucepan until bubbly and hot. Spoon half over corn chips in casserole. Top with half each of cheese, onion and green pepper. Repeat layering with remaining half of chili mixture, cheese, onion and green pepper.

3. Pour 1 cup boiling water over all. Arrange sausages in spoke fashion on top. Sprinkle with remaining crushed corn chips.

4. Bake at 375° F for 20 to 25 minutes, or until bubbly hot. *Serves 4.*

## ROAST BEEF HASH AND EGGS

¼ cup butter or margarine
½ cup chopped onion
one 15-ounce can roast
  beef hash
2 tablespoons ketchup
4 eggs
buttered toast points

1. Melt half of the butter or margarine in large skillet. Add onion and sauté for 5 minutes, or until tender.

2. Add roast beef hash and ketchup and heat thoroughly. Push to side of skillet.

3. Melt remaining butter or margarine in center of skillet. Add eggs, breaking up yolks. Scramble slightly and then mix together with meat mixture. Serve immediately with hot buttered toast points. *Serves 4.*

## LAZY DAY TAMALE DISH

2 tablespoons butter or
  margarine
½ cup chopped onion
½ cup chopped green
  pepper
one 16-ounce can beef
  tamales in sauce
one 16-ounce can cream-
  style corn
one 8-ounce can seasoned
  tomato sauce
½ to 1 teaspoon chili
  powder
¾ to 1 cup shredded sharp
  cheese
¼ cup sliced pitted ripe
  olives

1. Melt butter or margarine in large skillet. Add onion and green pepper; cook 3 or 4 minutes until soft. Stir in sauce drained from canned tamales.

2. Add corn, tomato sauce and chili powder. Mix well; simmer 5 minutes. Stir in ½ cup of the cheese.

3. Cut tamales in half lengthwise; arrange them cut side up on corn mixture. Heat thoroughly.

4. Sprinkle remaining cheese around edge of skillet; garnish with olives. *Serves 4.*

## BEAN AND BEEF BURGERS

one 8-ounce can pork and
  beans
two 3-ounce packages
  sliced smoked beef, cut in
  julienne strips
⅓ cup mayonnaise
2 tablespoons finely
  chopped onion
2 tablespoons pickle relish,
  drained
8 sesame seed hamburger
  buns
¾ cup shredded Cheddar
  cheese

1. Preheat broiler. In a medium-size shallow bowl, mash and stir beans. Add julienne strips of smoked beef and mayonnaise; mix well.

2. Mix in chopped onion and pickle relish. Spread mixture on bottom halves of hamburger buns; broil for 3 minutes.

3. Sprinkle each bun with cheese; return to broiler about 1 minute or just until cheese melts. Cover with top halves of hamburger buns and serve at once. *Serves 6 to 8.*

## BELGIAN CORNED BEEF

3 slices bacon
1 cup sliced mushrooms
two 3-ounce packages
    sliced corned beef
three 7/8-ounce packages
    brown gravy mix
two 5-ounce packages
    frozen waffles
butter

1. Fry bacon until crisp in medium skillet. Remove bacon to a paper towel to drain; crumble and set aside. Sauté mushrooms in remaining bacon fat.

2. Using two forks, pull beef into pieces; add to mushrooms in skillet.

3. Prepare gravy mix according to label directions. Stir into mushrooms and beef. Add crumbled bacon and keep hot.

4. Toast and butter the waffles; serve topped with beef mixture. *Serves 4.*

## EASY REUBEN SANDWICHES

one 12-ounce can corned
    beef, flaked
one 8-ounce can
    sauerkraut, rinsed,
    drained and chopped
1 cup shredded Swiss
    cheese
½ cup bottled Thousand
    Island dressing
1 teaspoon prepared
    mustard
8 large slices rye bread
butter or margarine

1. In large bowl, combine corned beef, sauerkraut, Swiss cheese, dressing and mustard until well blended.

2. Spoon mixture onto 4 slices of bread. Top with remaining slices of bread. Spread butter or margarine on outside of each sandwich.

3. Sauté sandwiches in a large skillet for 5 minutes, or until golden brown and crisp on both sides; sauté two sandwiches at a time, turning with a large spatula. *Serves 4.*

## VEAL CHAMPIGNON

1½ pounds veal scaloppine,
    cut into ¾-inch cubes
¼ cup flour
1 teaspoon salt
few pinches of pepper
2 tablespoons butter or
    margarine
2 cups sliced fresh
    mushrooms
¼ cup dry white wine
¼ cup water
2 tablespoons chopped
    chives
¼ teaspoon crumbled
    tarragon
hot cooked egg noodles

1. Dredge veal cubes in mixture of flour, salt and pepper on waxed paper.

2. Melt butter or margarine in a large skillet. Add veal and brown on all sides. Remove from skillet and set aside.

3. Sauté mushrooms in pan drippings for 3 minutes, or until tender. Stir in wine, water, chives and tarragon. Bring to boiling point; reduce heat.

4. Return veal to skillet and simmer for 15 minutes, covered, or until veal is tender when pierced with a fork. Serve over noodles. *Serves 4 to 6.*

*Note:* Instead of veal scaloppine, you can use 1½ pounds of veal shoulder, cut in thin slices. Tenderize each slice, using ¼ teaspoon instant meat tenderizer according to label directions. Cut into ¾ x ¾-inch pieces.

# SMOKED PORK CHOPS AND BRUSSELS SPROUTS

4 precooked smoked pork
  chops
1 tablespoon oil
¼ cup butter or margarine
⅓ cup flour
1 chicken bouillon cube
¾ cup boiling water
¾ cup light cream
one 10-ounce package
  frozen Brussels sprouts
1 cup sliced celery, in 1-inch
  slices
½ teaspoon salt
1 cup boiling water

1. In large skillet over medium heat, brown chops on both sides in hot oil. Remove from skillet and set aside. Heat butter or margarine in skillet; add flour. Stir and cook for about 1 minute.

2. Dissolve bouillon cube in ¾ cup boiling water; stir into flour mixture in skillet. Immediately stir in light cream. Mix over low heat until smooth and thickened.

3. Thaw Brussels sprouts; combine with celery, salt and 1 cup boiling water in a medium saucepan; cook 8 to 10 minutes or until sprouts are fork tender. Drain very well.

4. Add Brussels sprouts, celery and pork chops to sauce; heat through. *Serves 4.*

# GRILLED HAM WITH PEACH SAUCE

½ cup water
one 3-ounce package
  peach-flavored gelatin
¼ cup brown sugar, firmly
  packed
3 tablespoons lemon juice
1½- to 2-pound ham center
  slice, 1 inch thick
6 fresh or canned peach
  halves

1. Preheat broiler. In small saucepan, combine water, gelatin, brown sugar and lemon juice. Cook over medium heat, stirring constantly, until gelatin and sugar dissolve.

2. Grease broiler rack and line pan underneath with aluminum foil. Place ham on rack. Brush with peach glaze.

3. Broil 4 inches from heat, 10 minutes per side, basting occasionally with glaze.

4. Broil peach halves during last 5 minutes of broiling time, basting with glaze. *Serves 6.*

# HAM AND BISCUIT LOAF

1 pound sliced boiled ham
two 8-ounce packages
  refrigerator flaky biscuits
¼ cup mayonnaise or salad
  dressing
1 tablespoon prepared
  mustard
1 teaspoon crumbled
  oregano

1. Preheat oven to 400° F. Cut ham into 1 x 2-inch strips; set aside.

2. Unroll 1 package of biscuit dough onto lightly floured board. Roll out to a 12 x 7-inch rectangle.

3. Place dough on lightly greased cookie sheet and spread with mayonnaise or salad dressing. Top with an even layer of ham. Spread with mustard and sprinkle with oregano.

4. Roll out remaining package of biscuit dough and cut into strips. Place diagonally on top of ham, joining to bottom biscuit dough.

5. Bake 20 minutes, or until golden brown. Serve with your favorite cheese, if you wish. *Serves 6.*

## CHEESE-HAMWICHES

one 12-ounce package fully
    cooked ham patties
    (6 to a package)
6 hamburger rolls
mayonnaise or salad
    dressing
prepared mustard
6 slices process American
    cheese
1 large Bermuda onion,
    thinly sliced
lettuce

1. Sauté patties in a large skillet over medium heat, turning to brown both sides.

2. Split the hamburger rolls and toast under broiler. Spread bottom halves of rolls with mayonnaise or salad dressing, and mustard. Place browned patties on top, then American cheese slices.

3. Broil 3 inches from heat until cheese melts. Place onion slices, lettuce and top halves of rolls over bubbling cheese; serve immediately. *Serves 6.*

## KNOCKWURST AND BEANS

1 pound knockwurst
1 tablespoon vegetable oil
two 16-ounce cans pork
    and beans with tomato
    sauce
¼ cup ketchup
1 tablespoon prepared
    mustard
1 tablespoon Worcestershire
    sauce
1 tablespoon brown sugar
½ teaspoon liquid smoke

1. Cut knockwurst in half lengthwise; brown in hot oil in heavy skillet over medium heat.

2. Add beans; stir in ketchup, mustard, Worcestershire sauce, brown sugar and liquid smoke.

3. Simmer mixture over low heat until very hot and bubbly, about 15 minutes. *Serves 6.*

## SAUSAGE AND CHICKEN-NOODLE DINNER

one 6-ounce package
    brown-and-serve
    sausages
1 tablespoon butter or
    margarine
1 tablespoon flour
one 8-ounce can stewed
    tomatoes
one 15-ounce jar chicken-
    noodle dinner
¼ cup finely chopped onion
2 tablespoons finely
    chopped parsley

1. Brown sausages in large skillet over moderate heat. Remove and set aside. Add butter or margarine to drippings in skillet, swirling until melted. Stir in flour until well blended.

2. Add stewed tomatoes, crushing with spoon. Stir in chicken-noodle dinner, onion and parsley.

3. Bring to boiling point; lower heat and simmer 10 minutes, or until bubbly hot and slightly thickened. Return sausages to skillet. Continue simmering until sausages are heated through. *Serves 6.*

## SOUP-ER SUPPER

4 cups water
1½ cups milk
one 10¾-ounce can
  condensed cream of
  potato soup
one 10¾-ounce can
  condensed cream of
  mushroom soup
two 5-ounce cans Vienna
  sausages, halved
one 8¾-ounce can cream-
  style corn
one ¾-ounce envelope
  onion soup mix
crackers or French bread

1. In large saucepan, combine water, milk, condensed cream of potato and mushroom soups, Vienna sausage halves, corn and onion soup mix.

2. Bring almost to boiling point over medium heat, stirring frequently. Lower heat and simmer 10 minutes. Serve with crackers or French bread. *Serves 8.*

## QUICK CHEESE FRANKS

2 tablespoons butter or
  margarine
1 cup chopped onion
one 1-pound package
  frankfurters, cut into thirds
1 cup diced green pepper
one 10¾-ounce can
  condensed Cheddar
  cheese soup
½ cup milk
1 teaspoon prepared
  mustard
3 drops hot pepper sauce
hot cooked rice or noodles

1. Melt butter or margarine in large skillet over medium heat. Add onion and sauté until tender. Add frankfurters and green pepper. Cook 5 minutes longer.

2. Stir in condensed soup, milk, mustard and hot pepper sauce. Bring just to boiling point. Reduce heat and simmer 5 minutes. Serve over rice or noodles. *Serves 4.*

## CRISP AND SAVORY CASSEROLE

2 cups diced bologna
4 hard-cooked eggs, diced
¾ cup mayonnaise
½ cup sliced celery
¼ cup sliced stuffed green
  olives
¼ cup chopped onion
1 teaspoon prepared
  mustard
⅛ teaspoon pepper
1 cup crushed potato chips

1. In large bowl, combine bologna, eggs, mayonnaise, celery, olives, onion, mustard and pepper until well blended.

2. Place mixture in round 8-inch baking pan, greased. Sprinkle with crushed potato chips. Bake at 400° F for 25 minutes, or until bubbly hot and golden. *Serves 4.*

## PEPPERONI-VEGETABLE POT

2 cups water
½ teaspoon salt
2 medium potatoes
one 10-ounce package
  frozen cut green beans
½ pound pepperoni, thinly
  sliced
1 tablespoon vegetable oil
½ cup chopped onion
one 15-ounce jar marinara
  sauce

1.  Heat water to boiling point with ½ teaspoon salt in medium saucepan.

2.  Meanwhile, peel and cube potatoes; add to boiling water along with green beans. Boil over moderate heat 10 minutes, or until vegetables are just tender; drain and set aside.

3.  Brown pepperoni in hot oil in same saucepan; remove and set aside. Pour off all but 1 tablespoon drippings.

4.  Sauté onion in drippings 5 minutes, or until tender. Add marinara sauce and bring to boiling point. Lower heat and simmer 5 minutes.

5.  Return potatoes, beans and pepperoni to saucepan. Continue cooking until heated through, about 5 minutes. *Serves 4.*

## CRUSTY MEAT AND VEGETABLE ROLL-UP

⅔ cup milk
2 cups buttermilk biscuit
  mix
one 12-ounce can luncheon
  meat, finely diced
½ cup finely chopped celery
one 8-ounce can peas,
  drained
1 egg
one 10¾-ounce can
  condensed cream of
  mushroom soup
½ cup half-and-half or milk

1.  Preheat oven to 425° F.

2.  In medium bowl, add milk to biscuit mix to make a soft dough. Roll out to an 8 x 12-inch rectangle on lightly floured board.

3.  In small bowl, combine luncheon meat, celery, peas and egg until well blended. Spread mixture on dough, leaving a ½-inch border.

4.  Starting at narrow end, roll up jelly-roll fashion. Cut into 1½-inch slices. Place slices cut side down on a greased cookie sheet.

5.  Bake 20 minutes, or until golden. Serve with sauce made from condensed soup and half-and-half or milk, heated together until bubbly. *Serves 4.*

## TASTY TURKEY

1 tablespoon butter or
   margarine
1 cup sliced mushrooms
1 cup sliced onion
one 8-ounce can tomato
   sauce
1½ cups sliced zucchini
2 tablespoons chopped
   parsley
¾ teaspoon salt
½ teaspoon basil
1 cup unflavored yogurt
1 cup diced precooked
   turkey

1. Melt butter or margarine in large skillet; add mushrooms and sauté over medium heat. Stir in onion and cook 2 minutes. Add tomato sauce.

2. Add zucchini, parsley, salt and basil; cook 4 or 5 minutes until zucchini is crisp-tender. Stir occasionally to prevent sticking.

3. Reduce heat to low; stir in yogurt and turkey. Heat thoroughly, but do *not* boil. *Serves 4.*

## JAPANESE CHICKEN DELIGHT

2 whole chicken breasts,
   skinned and boned
¼ cup vegetable oil
1 cup sliced onion
1 cup julienne strips green
   pepper
one 10-ounce package
   frozen Japanese-style
   vegetables
1 quart boiling water
two 3-ounce packages
   Oriental noodle soup mix
   with seasonings

1. Pound the chicken breasts to flatten a little; then cut into strips. Heat oil in a large skillet or wok; add onion and green pepper. Sauté 3 or 4 minutes.

2. Push the onion and green pepper to one side; add the chicken strips. Cook and stir over moderate heat for about 10 minutes.

3. Add Japanese-style vegetables to 1 quart of boiling water and bring to the boiling point again. Add the noodles (reserve the seasoning packets) and boil rapidly for 1 or 2 minutes; drain very well.

4. Add drained vegetables and noodles to chicken in skillet. Sprinkle on the contents of the reserved seasoning packets and mix very well. Cover and heat through for about 2 minutes. *Serves 4.*

## ITALIAN CHICKEN BREASTS

4 large chicken breast
   halves
¼ cup bottled Italian
   dressing
½ cup Italian-flavored bread
   crumbs

1. Dip chicken breasts in Italian dressing; then roll completely in bread crumbs on a sheet of waxed paper.

2. Place on greased cookie sheet. Cover with foil.

3. Bake at 425° F for 25 minutes; uncover and bake 10 minutes longer, or until chicken is tender when pierced with a fork. *Serves 4.*

## CHICKEN ROLL PUFFS

4 frozen patty shells (from a 10-ounce package)
one 10¾-ounce can condensed cream of chicken soup
¾ cup milk
1 cup sour cream
¼ teaspoon paprika
1 pound precooked chicken roll, not sliced
chopped parsley

1. Preheat oven to 400° F. Arrange 4 patty shells on cookie sheet and bake according to label directions for 20 to 25 minutes, until puffed and golden; set aside to cool on a wire rack.

2. Combine condensed soup and milk in a large saucepan. Mix until smooth. Heat 1 minute; blend in sour cream and paprika.

3. Dice the chicken roll and add to hot sauce. Heat 3 or 4 minutes until very hot; do not simmer or boil or sauce will separate.

4. Lift out centers from patty shells and set aside. Fill patty shells with chicken and sauce. Replace centers and sprinkle with parsley. *Serves 4.*

*Note:* Return the 2 extra patty shells in package to freezer for later use.

## CHICKEN LIVER STROGANOFF

½ pound chicken livers, rinsed and patted dry
¼ cup flour
¼ cup butter or margarine
3 tablespoons vegetable oil
1½ cups thinly sliced onions
1 teaspoon paprika
½ teaspoon salt
⅛ teaspoon pepper
1 cup sour cream
hot cooked rice or noodles

1. Halve the chicken livers and dredge in flour on waxed paper. Melt butter or margarine in large skillet. Add the livers and brown quickly on all sides; remove and set aside.

2. Add oil to skillet. Sauté onions over moderate heat 5 minutes, or until tender. Stir in paprika, salt and pepper until well blended.

3. Return livers to skillet. Cover skillet and lower heat; simmer 15 minutes.

4. Add sour cream. Heat very gently, but do *not* boil. Serve over rice or noodles. *Serves 4.*

*TimeSaving Tip: Use kitchen scissors to snip chicken livers in half and to speedily remove surplus fat and membranes. It is important to rinse chicken livers well. To do this most efficiently, place in a large sieve under cold running water; shake well to drain before patting dry with paper towels. Remember, chicken livers can be a "free bonus" if collected from whole or quartered chicken (the livers are generally included in the package). Rinse well and freeze until ready to use; do not store longer than 6 months.*

## GUACAMOLE-CHICKEN SANDWICHES

½ cup sour cream
1 very ripe avocado, halved, peeled and pitted
1 teaspoon lemon juice
¼ teaspoon chili powder
pinch of garlic salt
8 slices white bread
1 cup shredded lettuce
½ pound precooked chicken or chicken roll, sliced
1 tomato, cut into 4 slices
2 slices bacon, crisply fried and crumbled
8 pitted ripe olives

1. In electric blender, puree sour cream, avocado, lemon juice, chili powder and garlic salt at high speed until very smooth.

2. Place bread on cookie sheet. Broil 3 inches from heat to toast bread on one side only.

3. Spread avocado mixture on untoasted sides of bread. Top 4 slices with shredded lettuce, then chicken and tomato slices. Sprinkle crumbled bacon over tomato slices. Top with remaining bread.

4. Cut sandwiches in half, diagonally. Spear olives with toothpicks. Insert into sandwiches to secure. *Serves 4.*

## NORWEGIAN FISH SOUP

¼ cup butter or margarine
2 cups sliced onions
½ cup grated carrot
½ cup thinly sliced celery
one 16-ounce package frozen fillet of flounder, haddock or cod, partially thawed
one 8-ounce bottle clam juice
one 8-ounce can minced clams
½ cup water
½ cup dry white wine
1 teaspoon dried dill
salt and pepper to taste
crusty bread or crackers

1. Melt butter or margarine in a large saucepan over low heat. Add onions and sauté 5 minutes, or until soft. Push to one side and add carrot and celery. Sauté 5 minutes.

2. Cut fish into 1-inch cubes; add to saucepan together with clam juice, minced clams and their liquid, water, wine and dill.

3. Bring slowly to boiling point. Lower heat and simmer 15 minutes. Taste and season with salt and pepper, if needed. Serve with crusty bread or crackers. *Serves 4 to 6.*

did not use the celery – very good.

# FISH STICKS WITH SOUR CREAM DRESSING

one 16-ounce package
   frozen fish sticks
½ cup sour cream
1 tablespoon vinegar
1 teaspoon sugar
1 teaspoon dried parsley
1 teaspoon minced green
   onion
½ teaspoon salt
¼ teaspoon crumbled dried
   dill
⅛ teaspoon paprika

1. Bake fish sticks according to label directions.

2. Combine sour cream, vinegar, sugar, parsley, green onion, salt, dill and paprika in a small bowl until well blended. Let stand while fish sticks bake.

3. Spoon sour cream sauce over fish sticks. Serve immediately. *Serves 4.*

# QUICK SALMON CROQUETTES

one 15½-ounce can pink or
   red salmon
2 tablespoons finely
   chopped onion
1 tablespoon finely chopped
   parsley
1 teaspoon chopped chives
¼ teaspoon salt
½ cup quick-cooking
   oatmeal
1 egg, beaten
3 or 4 tablespoons ketchup
⅓ cup flour
½ cup vegetable oil

1. Preheat oven to 300° F. Drain salmon, reserving liquid. Flake salmon into a medium bowl, discarding bones.

2. Add onion, parsley, chives, salt and oatmeal; mix well and let stand 10 minutes. Mix beaten egg with reserved salmon liquid; blend into salmon mixture.

3. Add enough ketchup to mixture to make it moist but easy to handle. Shape salmon mixture into 12 small log shapes (croquettes); roll lightly in flour.

4. Heat oil in a medium skillet. Add croquettes and brown quickly. Drain on paper towels.

5. Transfer browned croquettes to a shallow casserole or baking dish. Bake 8 to 10 minutes. *Serves 4 to 6.*

*TimeSaving Tip: Flake salmon with ease with a fork; remove not only the bones but any skin that seems unusually dark. The fastest way to shape croquettes is to roll the entire salmon mixture into a long roll on a lightly floured board; divide evenly into 12 pieces and roll each piece between lightly floured hands. To save both time and energy, bake salmon croquettes on the greased tray of a toaster oven; these small countertop ovens take only 2 minutes to preheat.*

## CLAM FRITTERS

1 cup milk
2 eggs, separated
2 tablespoons butter or
   margarine, melted
1 teaspoon salt
1 cup flour
two 6½-ounce cans minced
   clams, well drained
vegetable oil
tartar sauce

1. In medium bowl, beat milk, egg yolks, melted butter or margarine, and salt until well blended. Sift flour over top; beat into milk mixture.

2. Beat egg whites with electric mixer at high speed until stiff peaks form. Fold into batter. Add well-drained clams.

3. Pour oil to a depth of 2 inches in a large skillet. Insert deep-fat thermometer and heat oil to 375° F. (If you don't have a deep-fat thermometer, drop a cube of day-old bread into fat; temperature is about 375° F when cube browns in 60 seconds.)

4. Drop batter by tablespoons, 4 or 5 at a time, into hot fat. Fry until lightly browned on both sides. Drain on heated serving plate, lined with paper towels. Keep warm while frying remaining batter. Serve with tartar sauce. *Serves 4.*

## SCALLOP AND BROCCOLI STIR-FRY

2 tablespoons cold water
2 teaspoons cornstarch
1 teaspoon sugar
1 envelope powdered beef
   concentrate
¼ teaspoon salt
½ cup dry sherry or dry
   white wine
2 tablespoons vegetable oil
one 8-ounce can bamboo
   shoots, drained
1 cup sliced onion
1 cup sliced fresh
   mushrooms
one 10-ounce package
   frozen broccoli
one 12-ounce package
   frozen scallops
boiling water
½ teaspoon salt
soy sauce to taste

1. Blend 2 tablespoons cold water with cornstarch in a small saucepan; stir in sugar, beef concentrate, salt, and sherry or white wine. Simmer and stir over low heat until clear and thickened. Cover and set aside.

2. Heat oil in large skillet or wok. Add drained bamboo shoots, onion and mushrooms; stir-fry until just crisp-tender, about 3 minutes. Remove from skillet and keep warm.

3. Combine frozen broccoli and frozen scallops in medium saucepan. Add boiling water to cover and ½ teaspoon salt. Return water to boiling point over high heat.

4. Drain broccoli and scallops immediately, then turn into the hot skillet; if necessary, add a little more oil. Cook over high heat for 4 or 5 minutes, stirring constantly.

5. Return bamboo shoots, onion and mushrooms to skillet; stir in reserved wine mixture. Cook and stir until hot and bubbly. Add soy sauce. *Serves 4.*

# SHRIMP WITH CHINESE VEGETABLES

1 pound frozen shrimp, thawed, shelled and deveined
2 tablespoons margarine or oil
1 cup diagonally sliced celery
2 cups sliced onions
one 9-ounce package frozen leaf spinach, thawed
one 16-ounce can mixed Chinese vegetables, drained
one 13¾-ounce can chicken broth
¼ cup soy sauce
2 tablespoons cornstarch
½ teaspoon garlic powder
¼ teaspoon pepper
hot cooked rice

1. In a large skillet or wok, sauté shrimp in melted margarine or hot oil until shrimp turn pink. Add celery and onions; cook and stir 3 to 5 minutes.

2. Drain spinach and add to skillet; stir in mixed vegetables.

3. Blend together chicken broth, soy sauce, cornstarch, garlic powder and pepper in a small saucepan. Simmer over low heat until sauce begins to clear and thicken.

4. Add sauce to skillet. Cook and stir about 2 minutes until sauce is clear. Serve over fluffy rice. *Serves 6.*

# LOBSTER NEWBURG

4 frozen patty shells (from a 10-ounce package)
¼ cup butter or margarine
2 tablespoons flour
1½ cups light cream
3 egg yolks
one 5-ounce can lobster, drained
¼ cup dry white wine
1 teaspoon lemon juice
salt to taste
paprika

1. Bake 4 patty shells according to label directions.

2. Heat butter or margarine in a medium skillet; blend in flour over low heat. Cook until bubbly. Gradually stir in cream; cook and stir over low heat until sauce thickens and boils.

3. Beat egg yolks until frothy. Stir a small amount of hot sauce into beaten egg yolks, then stir all back into the hot sauce.

4. Cook over low heat, stirring constantly until thickened. Cut lobster into small pieces, removing all cartilage. Add to sauce along with wine, lemon juice and salt. Gently heat through.

5. Sprinkle with paprika and serve in baked patty shells. *Serves 4.*

*Note:* Return the 2 extra patty shells in package to freezer for later use.

## EASY CRABMEAT MORNAY

½ cup butter or margarine
½ cup chopped green onions (white part only)
½ cup finely chopped parsley
2 tablespoons flour
2 cups half-and-half or light cream
2 cups shredded Swiss cheese
1 tablespoon dry white wine
one 6½-ounce can crabmeat, drained and cartilage removed

1. Melt butter or margarine in skillet; add green onions and parsley and sauté. Stir in flour; cook for 2 minutes.

2. Stir in half-and-half or light cream; cook and stir until smooth and blended.

3. Stir in shredded cheese, a handful at a time. When cheese is completely melted and sauce is blended and smooth, stir in wine and crabmeat. *Serves 4.*

*Note:* This dish makes an excellent hors d'oeuvre served from a chafing dish with melba toast fingers.

## EASY SEAFOOD ROLL-UPS

one 7-ounce can tuna, drained
one 6½-ounce can crabmeat, drained and cartilage removed
½ cup grated Swiss or Cheddar cheese
1 tablespoon finely chopped onion
1 teaspoon celery salt
one 8-ounce package refrigerator crescent rolls

1. Preheat oven to 375° F. In medium bowl, combine tuna, crabmeat, cheese, onion and celery salt until well blended.

2. Separate crescent rolls. Flatten each one slightly. Place ¼ cup seafood mixture on each roll. Roll up, starting from wide end.

3. Place roll-ups on ungreased cookie sheet, point side down. Bake 12 to 15 minutes, or until golden brown. *Serves 4.*

## STIR-FRY TUNA

two 7-ounce cans tuna in oil
3 tablespoons butter or margarine
1 cup chopped green onions
1 green pepper, seeded and sliced
1 sweet red pepper, seeded and sliced
2 large celery ribs, sliced on the diagonal
2 cups sliced mushrooms
¼ cup soy sauce
hot buttered egg noodles

1. Drain the oil from tuna into a large skillet (or use a wok if available); reserve tuna. Add butter or margarine to oil and heat over medium heat.

2. Stir green onions, green and red pepper, celery and mushrooms into hot oil. Cook and stir for about 5 minutes.

3. Add tuna and soy sauce. Cook and stir 3 minutes longer. Serve over hot buttered egg noodles. *Serves 4.*

# MADRAS TUNA SANDWICHES

one 7-ounce can tuna,
  drained and flaked
½ cup mayonnaise or salad
  dressing
½ cup finely chopped celery
½ cup flaked coconut
¼ cup finely chopped
  almonds
1 tablespoon lemon juice
½ teaspoon curry powder
⅛ teaspoon pepper
8 slices bread

1. In medium bowl, combine tuna, mayonnaise or salad dressing, celery, coconut, almonds, lemon juice, curry powder and pepper until well blended.

2. Spread mixture on bread slices. Broil 4 inches from heat until bubbly hot and lightly golden. *Serves 4.*

# YOGURT "QUICHE"

1½ cups finely chopped
  cooked ham
1 cup unflavored yogurt
½ cup shredded Swiss
  cheese
8 saltine crackers, finely
  crushed
2 tablespoons butter or
  margarine, melted
1 tablespoon finely chopped
  onion
½ teaspoon caraway seeds
6 eggs

1. Preheat oven to 400° F.

2. In medium bowl, combine ham, yogurt, cheese, cracker crumbs, butter or margarine, onion and caraway seeds.

3. In small bowl of electric mixer, beat eggs at high speed, until thick and lemon colored. Fold into yogurt mixture until well blended. Pour into a greased 9 x 9 x 2-inch baking pan.

4. Bake 20 minutes, or until puffy and evenly browned. Cut into squares and serve hot. *Serves 4.*

# EGGS GRUYERE

2 medium onions, thinly
  sliced
⅓ cup butter or margarine
⅓ cup flour
1½ teaspoons salt
¼ teaspoon pepper
3 cups milk
⅔ cup evaporated milk or
  light cream
¾ cup shredded Gruyère
  cheese
8 hard-cooked eggs, sliced
hot cooked rice, toast
  points or muffins

1. In a large heavy saucepan over medium heat, sauté onions in butter or margarine until soft and very lightly colored. Stir in flour, salt and pepper; cook and stir until mixture bubbles.

2. Gradually stir in milk and evaporated milk or light cream. Cook and stir over medium-low heat until sauce is smooth and thickened.

3. Reduce heat to low and add the cheese. Stir until cheese is melted. Add the sliced eggs. Heat thoroughly, moving the egg slices about very carefully to prevent breaking.

4. When mixture is hot, serve on rice, buttered toast points or toasted English muffins. *Serves 6 to 8.*

## RAREBIT ON TOAST

4 cups grated sharp
   Cheddar cheese
2 teaspoons dry mustard
1 teaspoon Worcestershire
   sauce
½ teaspoon salt
one 7-ounce can evaporated
   milk, or 1 cup light cream
4 slices luncheon ham
4 slices toast
4 slices tomato
paprika

1. In medium skillet, combine Cheddar cheese, dry mustard, Worcestershire sauce and salt. Slowly stir in evaporated milk or light cream. Cook over moderate heat, stirring constantly, until cheese melts and sauce thickens.

2. Place ham slices on toast; pour sauce over ham. Top with tomato slices, then a sprinkling of paprika. Serve immediately. *Serves 4.*

## WELSH RAREBIT WITH MUSHROOMS

1 tablespoon butter or
   margarine
2 cups sliced mushrooms
¾ cup light cream
1 teaspoon Worcestershire
   sauce
½ teaspoon prepared
   mustard
⅛ teaspoon paprika
2 teaspoons flour
2 cups shredded sharp
   Cheddar cheese
buttered toast points

1. Melt butter or margarine in a medium saucepan; add mushrooms and sauté for 3 to 5 minutes. Add light cream, Worcestershire sauce, mustard and paprika.

2. Heat sauce mixture over low heat. Mix flour with cheese. Sprinkle sauce with ⅓ cup of the cheese mixture; stir in until melted. Continue adding cheese until all of it is incorporated into the sauce.

3. When cheese is melted and sauce is smooth and hot, pour over toast points. *Serves 4. (Shown on page 49.)*

## WINE-CHEESE TOAST

one 8-ounce loaf French
   bread
2 tablespoons butter or
   margarine
1½ tablespoons flour
½ cup milk
½ cup grated Cheddar,
   Gruyère or Swiss cheese
1 egg, beaten
1 tablespoon dry white wine
⅛ teaspoon garlic powder
⅛ teaspoon salt
⅛ teaspoon pepper
pinch of nutmeg
cooked ham or bacon

1. Cut bread diagonally into 10 slices. Place slices on cookie sheet. Broil 3 inches from heat to toast on one side only. Remove bread, but do not turn off broiler.

2. Melt butter or margarine in small saucepan. Stir in flour to form a smooth paste. Gradually stir in milk. Cook, stirring constantly, until mixture thickens and bubbles, about 3 minutes. Let cool a few minutes.

3. Stir in cheese, beaten egg, wine, garlic powder, salt, pepper and nutmeg until well blended. Spread 1 to 2 tablespoons cheese mixture on untoasted sides of bread.

4. Broil 4 inches from heat until bubbly hot and slightly brown. Serve immediately, accompanied with ham or bacon. *Serves 4.*

## QUICK BLINTZ SANDWICHES

one 12-ounce container
    creamed cottage cheese,
    drained
4 eggs
¼ cup sugar
12 slices bread
⅓ cup milk
¼ cup butter or margarine
strawberry jam

1. In small bowl, beat together cottage cheese, one of the eggs and the sugar until well blended. Spread about ¼ cup cheese mixture on each of 6 slices bread. Cover with remaining bread.

2. In pie plate, beat the remaining 3 eggs with milk until well blended. Dip sandwiches into egg mixture.

3. Melt half of the butter or margarine in large skillet. Brown half of the sandwiches on both sides. Remove to a heated serving platter and keep warm. Repeat with remaining butter or margarine and sandwiches. Serve with strawberry jam. *Serves 6.*

## GREEN AND GOLD MACARONI

one 7¼-ounce package
    macaroni and cheese
    dinner
2 tablespoons butter or
    margarine
½ cup chopped onion
3 tablespoons chopped
    green pepper
one 5-ounce can boned
    chicken, diced
¼ cup milk
1 tablespoon chopped
    chives

1. Prepare macaroni and cheese dinner according to label directions.

2. Meanwhile, melt butter or margarine in small skillet over medium heat. Sauté onion and green pepper 3 to 5 minutes, or until tender.

3. Add sautéed vegetables to cooked macaroni mixture, along with diced chicken, milk and chives. Mix well, and cook over moderate heat until bubbly hot. *Serves 4.*

## MACARONI "PLUS" SALAD

1 cup elbow macaroni,
    cooked, drained and
    cooled
1½ cups diced cooked ham
    or picnic shoulder
1 cup diced sharp Cheddar
    cheese
½ cup mayonnaise
2 hard-cooked eggs, diced
½ cup sliced celery
⅓ cup chopped green onions
¼ cup pickle relish, drained
2 tablespoons chopped
    pimiento
¼ teaspoon salt

1. Combine cooled macaroni, cooked ham, cheese and mayonnaise in a large serving bowl.

2. Add eggs, celery, green onions, pickle relish, pimiento and salt.

3. Fold in gently to prevent ingredients from breaking up. Taste and add seasoning if necessary. Chill. *Serves 4.*

## ITALIAN PASTA POTPOURRI

1 pound Italian sausages
1 cup sliced fresh
  mushrooms
1 tablespoon olive or
  vegetable oil
one 8-ounce package thin
  spaghetti
boiling salted water
2 eggs
½ cup grated Parmesan
  cheese
¼ cup milk
1 teaspoon crumbled basil
½ teaspoon salt
¼ teaspoon garlic powder
¼ cup butter or margarine

1. Pour water to depth of ½ inch in large skillet. Prick sausages and add to skillet. Cook uncovered over medium-high heat 20 minutes, adding water if necessary. Drain and cut into 1-inch pieces; set aside.

2. In same skillet, sauté mushrooms in hot oil for 3 minutes, or until tender; set aside.

3. In large saucepan, cook spaghetti in boiling salted water according to label directions. In small bowl, beat eggs slightly; add cheese, milk, basil, salt and garlic powder.

4. Drain spaghetti well. Return to saucepan. Add butter or margarine and toss gently until completely melted. Add reserved sausage, mushrooms and egg mixture. Toss gently until thoroughly blended and serve immediately. *Serves 6. (Shown on page 50.)*

## PEPPERONI PASTA

¼ cup olive or vegetable oil
½ pound pepperoni, thinly
  sliced
1½ cups julienne strips
  green pepper
1 cup sliced onion
½ teaspoon garlic powder
one 15-ounce can stewed
  tomatoes
one 8-ounce can tomato
  sauce
1 teaspoon crumbled
  oregano
½ teaspoon salt
one 1-pound package thin
  spaghetti
boiling salted water
½ cup grated Parmesan
  cheese

1. Heat oil in a skillet over medium heat. Add pepperoni, green pepper, onion and garlic powder. Cook, stirring frequently, for 5 minutes, or until onion slices and pepper strips are tender.

2. Stir in stewed tomatoes, tomato sauce, oregano and salt. Bring mixture to boiling point; cover skillet and lower heat. Simmer sauce while preparing spaghetti, uncovering sauce during last few moments to thicken slightly.

3. Cook spaghetti in boiling salted water according to label directions. Drain well and place on heated serving platter. Spoon sauce over and sprinkle with cheese. *Serves 6.*

## FETTUCCINE ALFREDO

1 cup heavy cream
1 cup butter, softened
one 12-ounce package
   fettuccine
boiling salted water
¾ cup grated Parmesan
   cheese
¼ cup finely chopped
   parsley

1. Using electric mixer at high speed, beat heavy cream in medium bowl until medium-stiff peaks form. Beat in the very soft butter until well blended. (This may be done early in the day; cover and refrigerate until serving time.)

2. Cook fettuccine in boiling salted water according to label directions. Drain well and place in large serving bowl.

3. Sprinkle half of the cheese over fettuccine. Add half of the butter mixture and toss gently. Add remaining cheese and toss. Add remaining butter mixture and parsley. Toss again. *Serves 6.*

## STUFFED PITA BREAD

one 15-ounce can chick peas
2 tablespoons water
¼ cup chopped onion
1 clove garlic, crushed
1 tablespoon vegetable oil
½ cup sesame spread
½ cup toasted sesame seeds
4 rounds pita bread
shredded lettuce
grated cheese
sliced ripe olives
chopped tomatoes
chopped dill pickles
chopped hot peppers

1. Drain chick peas, reserving 3 tablespoons liquid. Place chick peas, reserved liquid and 2 tablespoons water in electric blender. Cover and process at high speed until smooth.

2. In small skillet, sauté onion and garlic in hot oil for 3 minutes, or until tender but not brown.

3. In large bowl, combine pureed chick peas, sautéed onion and garlic, sesame spread and sesame seeds until well blended.

4. Cut a 4-inch slit around edge of each pita round to form an open "pocket." Fill with chick pea mixture and let each person choose remaining sandwich accompaniments. *Serves 4.*

*Note:* Sesame spread (tahini) can be found in many gourmet shops or specialty stores with a Middle Eastern flavor.

## CORN AND TOMATO CHOWDER

3 slices bacon
1 cup sliced celery
½ cup finely chopped onion
3 tablespoons flour
1 teaspoon salt
¼ teaspoon pepper
4 cups milk
one 16-ounce can corn
one 16-ounce can stewed
   tomatoes
1 teaspoon Worcestershire
   sauce

1. Fry bacon until crisp in a large saucepan. Remove bacon to a paper towel to drain; crumble and set aside. Add celery and onion to bacon fat remaining in saucepan; cook for 2 or 3 minutes.

2. Blend in flour, salt and pepper. Stir in milk; cook until mixture begins to thicken, stirring constantly.

3. Add corn, tomatoes and Worcestershire sauce. Mix very well; heat thoroughly. Sprinkle with crumbled bacon. Serve piping hot with crisp whole wheat crackers. *Serves 4 as a main dish.*

# FORTY-FIVE MINUTE MAIN COURSES

CHAPTER — TWO

**F**rom the initial turn of the oven dial to the first delicious mouthful, these main courses take no more than 45 minutes. What difference does an extra 15 minutes make? Is it worth spending this additional time when you can produce attractive and tasty main dishes in just 30 minutes? It's more than worthwhile when you consider what those extra 15 minutes will give you:

- More substantial main dishes. There is time to make an oven-baked Shepherd's Pie, a flavorful Skillet Lasagne, a hearty Italian Chicken Sauté.
- More sophisticated entrées. There's time to make a sauce that might go awry if hurried, time to slowly simmer Veal Roulades, and time to bake Creamy Piquant Bluefish to perfection.
- Important accompaniments will be ready as well as the main dish. There is time to bake crisp, puff-pastry shells for Creamed Turkey, saffron-seasoned rice for Creamy Ground Veal, hot buttered noodles for Hamburger Stroganoff.
- You'll often have time to prepare the rest of the meal as well. A healthful salad such as spinach or watercress with chunks of tomato, a piping hot beef bouillon, or a simple and satisfying fruit dessert can be assembled in these few extra minutes.

So take another look at the clock, then pick a recipe from this chapter. In just 45 minutes you can have a magnificent meal.

## STEAK WITH BLACK BUTTER

⅓ cup butter or margarine
1 tablespoon lemon juice
1 teaspoon salt
¼ cup blanched almonds, coarsely chopped
one 2- to 2½-pound sirloin steak, about 1½ inches thick

1. Preheat broiler. Melt butter or margarine in small saucepan over medium heat. Stir in lemon juice and salt. Cook until butter or margarine begins to brown.

2. Turn heat to low; add almonds. Keep on a simmer while preparing steak.

3. Place steak on greased rack in broiler pan; broil 7 to 10 minutes per side.

4. When steak is done, place on heated platter. Pour browned butter sauce over the steak and serve at once. *Serves 4 to 6.*

## CUBE STEAKS BEARNAISE

4 beef cube steaks
salt and pepper to taste
1 tablespoon brown steak sauce
one 6-ounce jar Béarnaise sauce

1. Preheat broiler. Sprinkle both sides of steaks with salt and pepper; brush both sides with steak sauce. Let stand 2 or 3 minutes.

2. Heat Béarnaise sauce in top of double boiler over simmering water.

3. Broil steaks about 3 inches from heat, 2 minutes per side. Top each steak with Béarnaise sauce and serve at once. *Serves 4.*

## CUBE STEAK WITH COGNAC SAUCE

2 tablespoons butter or margarine
½ teaspoon crumbled rosemary
4 beef cube steaks (½ pound each)
3 tablespoons Cognac or beef broth
¼ teaspoon Worcestershire sauce
¼ teaspoon dry mustard

1. Melt 1 tablespoon of the butter or margarine in large skillet over low heat; add rosemary. Do not let butter or margarine brown, but cook until it is well flavored with the rosemary.

2. Add cube steaks and cook until done, turning often. Remove to hot platter and keep warm.

3. Add remaining tablespoon butter or margarine to skillet. Add Cognac or broth, Worcestershire sauce and dry mustard to skillet. Heat, but do *not* boil. Pour over steaks. *Serves 4.*

## SUKIYAKI

1½ pounds sirloin steak
one 10¾-ounce can beef
   broth
⅓ cup soy sauce
2 tablespoons sugar
1 cup sliced onion
1 cup julienne strips green
   pepper
1 cup julienne strips celery
2 cups sliced mushrooms
2 bunches green onions, cut
   into 2-inch pieces
   (2 cups)
1 pound fresh spinach,
   rinsed
two 7-ounce cans bamboo
   shoots, drained and sliced

1. Trim fat from steak, reserving some of the fat. Cut steak across the grain into bite-size pieces.

2. Melt reserved fat in wok or large skillet over moderately low heat. Remove crisp pieces with slotted spoon. Add steak pieces and cook, stirring gently, until lightly browned.

3. In medium bowl, combine beef broth, soy sauce and sugar. Add half of the mixture to wok along with onion, green pepper and celery. Cook quickly, stirring frequently, for 5 minutes. Add more beef broth mixture as needed.

4. Stir in sliced mushrooms and green onions; cook 1 minute. Add spinach and bamboo shoots; cook 1 minute longer, or until steak and vegetables are tender. *Serves 6.*

## ASPARAGUS AND BEEF STIR-FRY

¼ cup vegetable oil
1 clove garlic
1 pound flank steak, cut
   into 2½-inch strips
   (¼ inch thick)
2 tablespoons soy sauce
2 tablespoons sherry
2 tablespoons steak sauce
1 pound asparagus,
   trimmed and cut
   diagonally into ½-inch
   slices
⅓ cup beef broth
1 tablespoon cornstarch
2 tablespoons water
¼ cup chopped red pepper
   (optional)
hot cooked rice

1. Heat 2 tablespoons of the oil in large skillet or wok. Add the garlic clove and brown it; remove garlic from skillet and discard.

2. Add steak strips and stir-fry quickly until almost brown. Remove to a heated plate.

3. In small bowl, combine soy sauce, sherry and steak sauce. Add to skillet with the remaining 2 tablespoons oil.

4. Add asparagus to skillet and stir-fry for 2 minutes, or until crisp-tender. Add beef broth; lower heat, cover and simmer asparagus for 3 minutes, or until tender.

5. In 1-cup measure, blend cornstarch and water. Add cornstarch mixture and beef strips to skillet. Cook, stirring gently, just until sauce thickens and bubbles. Garnish with chopped red pepper, if desired. Serve with rice. *Serves 4.* (Shown on page 51.)

## PEPPER STEAK

1½ pounds flank steak
½ cup butter or margarine
2 cups julienne strips green
   pepper
2 cups onion rings
2 cups sliced mushrooms
1 small clove garlic, crushed
1½ cups beef broth
2 tablespoons cornstarch
2 tablespoons soy sauce
1 teaspoon seasoned salt
½ teaspoon pepper
¾ cup red wine
3 small tomatoes, quartered
hot cooked rice

1. Slice steak across the grain into long thin strips. Melt half the butter or margarine in a 12-inch wok or skillet; add steak strips and sauté. Remove steak and set aside.

2. Melt remaining butter or margarine in same wok; add and sauté green pepper, onion rings, mushrooms and garlic. Add broth and bring to boiling point. Reduce heat; simmer 8 to 10 minutes.

3. Mix in cornstarch, soy sauce, salt, pepper and wine. Cook and stir over medium heat until thickened. Return steak strips to the wok and add tomatoes. Stir and simmer for 5 or 6 minutes.

4. Spoon over hot fluffy rice or wild rice mixture. *Serves 4.*

## BUDGET BEEF STEAK STEW

3 tablespoons flour
½ teaspoon salt
¼ teaspoon pepper
4 beef cube steaks, cut in
   ½ x 2-inch strips
3 tablespoons vegetable
   shortening
1 cup chopped onion
4 medium potatoes, peeled
   and cut in eighths
½ cup chopped fresh
   tomato
one 8-ounce can tomato
   sauce
1 teaspoon salt
⅛ teaspoon pepper
½ teaspoon garlic powder
one 10-ounce package
   frozen peas, thawed
chopped parsley

1. In large, clean brown paper or plastic bag, mix flour, ½ teaspoon salt and ¼ teaspoon pepper to make seasoned flour; add beef strips and shake vigorously until beef is well coated with flour.

2. Heat shortening in Dutch oven; add beef strips and brown. Add onion, potatoes, tomato and tomato sauce; bring to boiling point.

3. Reduce heat to low, stir in 1 teaspoon salt, ⅛ teaspoon pepper and the garlic powder. Simmer for 30 minutes. Stir occasionally to prevent sticking.

4. Add peas and cook over medium heat until peas are tender, about 5 minutes. Sprinkle with chopped parsley and serve. *Serves 4.*

## CHEESE-STEAK SANDWICHES

2 tablespoons bacon
   drippings or vegetable oil
1 cup chopped onion
one 14-ounce package
   frozen beef sandwich
   steaks
4 large soft rolls, split
butter or margarine
4 slices American cheese
1 medium tomato, cut in
   4 slices

1. Heat bacon drippings or vegetable oil in large skillet. Sauté onion until soft and golden, about 5 minutes.

2. Push onion to side of skillet; add frozen steaks and fry quickly, turning once. Toast and butter the rolls.

3. Place several pieces of fried steak on the bottom half of each roll. Top with a spoonful of sautéed onion, then a slice of cheese. Broil until cheese is partially melted. Cover with slice of tomato and top half of roll. *Serves 4.*

## HASH 'N' EGGS

1 tablespoon bacon fat,
   butter or margarine
one 15-ounce can corned
   beef hash
4 eggs
salt and pepper to taste
¼ cup chopped parsley

1. Heat bacon fat, butter or margarine in a large skillet. Turn hash into skillet and break up with a fork. Cook and turn over medium heat for 8 to 10 minutes.

2. Spread hash to cover bottom of skillet; flatten into an even layer. Mark hash into 4 sections. Break an egg on top of each section. Sprinkle with salt and pepper.

3. Cover skillet and cook over medium heat until eggs are done (eggs will look "poached"). Sprinkle with chopped parsley. *Serves 4.*

## SHEPHERDS' PIE

1 pound ground beef
2 tablespoons finely
   chopped onion
½ teaspoon seasoned salt
½ teaspoon pepper
1 teaspoon brown steak
   sauce
one 10-ounce package
   frozen peas, carrots and
   onions in butter sauce,
   thawed
one 4-ounce package
   instant potato flakes
butter or margarine

1. Brown ground beef with onion, salt, pepper and steak sauce in a medium skillet over low heat. Mix in thawed vegetables. Turn into a greased 8 x 8-inch baking dish.

2. Prepare instant mashed potatoes according to label directions for 6 servings. Spread over meat filling; swirl top. Dot with butter or margarine.

3. Bake at 350° F for 20 to 25 minutes, or until top browns. *Serves 4.*

## MY MOTHER'S MEAT LOAF

1 pound ground chuck
¾ cup quick-cooking
  oatmeal
½ cup chopped celery
½ cup chopped onion
1 tablespoon prepared mild
  mustard
1 egg
1 teaspoon mixed Italian
  herbs
½ teaspoon salt
¼ teaspoon pepper
1 cup ketchup or tomato
  sauce
½ teaspoon oregano

1. In large bowl, combine ground chuck, oatmeal, celery, onion and mustard; add egg. Mix very well using hands or large kitchen spoon.

2. Mix in Italian herbs, salt and pepper. Mixture should be firm and easy to handle. Turn into greased 13 x 9 x 2-inch baking dish. Shape mixture into oval loaf; score top into pattern of 1-inch diamonds.

3. Pour ketchup or tomato sauce over meat loaf; sprinkle with oregano. Bake at 375° F for 45 minutes, occasionally spooning sauce from bottom of dish over loaf. *Serves 4.*

## HAMBURGER STROGANOFF

1 pound ground beef
butter or margarine
½ cup finely chopped onion
1 clove garlic, crushed
2 cups sliced mushrooms
2 tablespoons flour
2 teaspoons salt
¼ teaspoon pepper
one 10¾-ounce can
  condensed cream of
  chicken soup
1 cup sour cream
one 10-ounce package
  frozen baby peas, thawed
hot buttered noodles

1. Shape ground beef into large patty. Brown patty in large skillet, 5 minutes per side; crumble into small pieces and then remove with slotted spoon to paper towel.

2. Add enough butter or margarine to drippings to make ¼ cup. Add onion and garlic and sauté for 3 to 5 minutes, or until tender but not brown. Push to side of skillet.

3. Add mushrooms to skillet and cook for 3 minutes, or until soft. Stir in flour, salt and pepper. Cook 2 minutes longer.

4. Add condensed chicken soup; bring to boiling point. Lower heat. Return ground beef to skillet; simmer 10 minutes, stirring occasionally.

5. Stir in sour cream and thawed peas. Heat 5 minutes, but do *not* boil. Serve over noodles. *Serves 4.*

## HAMBURGER AND CHEESE WITH NOODLES

one 16-ounce package fine
   noodles or thin spaghetti
boiling water
1 cup small curd cottage
   cheese or ricotta
one 8-ounce package cream
   cheese, softened
1 cup sour cream
½ cup finely chopped onion
1 pound ground chuck
one 15-ounce jar spaghetti
   sauce
1 cup tomato juice
2 tablespoons butter or
   margarine, melted
½ cup shredded mozzarella
   cheese

1. Cook noodles or spaghetti in boiling water according to label directions; drain and set aside.

2. In a large bowl, combine and mix cottage cheese or ricotta, softened cream cheese, sour cream and onion. Set aside.

3. Brown ground chuck in large skillet until all pink disappears. Stir in spaghetti sauce and tomato juice; cover and simmer for 8 to 10 minutes.

4. Layer ingredients in a lightly greased 2½-quart casserole as follows: half the cooked noodles or spaghetti; the cheese and sour cream mixture; the 2 tablespoons melted butter or margarine; the ground chuck mixture; the remaining noodles or spaghetti; and finally the shredded mozzarella cheese.

5. Bake at 375° F for 40 minutes or until cheese melts and browns, and mixture bubbles. *Serves 4.*

## SKILLET LASAGNE

1 pound ground beef
2 tablespoons butter or
   margarine
one ¾-ounce package
   spaghetti sauce mix
one 16-ounce container
   small curd cottage cheese
half of 16-ounce package
   uncooked broad lasagne
   noodles
2 tablespoons chopped
   parsley
2 teaspoons basil
1 teaspoon salt
one 16-ounce can tomatoes
one 8-ounce can tomato
   sauce
1 cup water
one 8-ounce package sliced
   mozzarella cheese, cut in
   julienne strips

1. Shape ground beef into a large flat patty. Melt butter or margarine in a 12-inch skillet; add patty and brown well on both sides. Break up and crumble patty with a fork; continue to cook until all pink disappears.

2. Sprinkle meat with half the spaghetti sauce mix. Spoon cottage cheese over meat. Layer noodles over cottage cheese.

3. Sprinkle noodles with remaining spaghetti sauce mix, and the parsley, basil and salt.

4. Pour tomatoes, tomato sauce and 1 cup water over all. Spread with the back of a spoon to assure that all ingredients are moistened.

5. Bring to boiling point; reduce heat to low. Cover skillet and simmer for 35 to 40 minutes, or until noodles are tender. Sprinkle mozzarella cheese over top; cover and let stand for 5 minutes. *Serves 4.*

## QUICK QUICK CHILI

1 pound ground beef
½ cup chopped onion
1 clove garlic, crushed
one 16-ounce can kidney
    beans, drained
one 16-ounce can tomatoes
1 tablespoon chili powder
1½ teaspoons salt
¼ teaspoon pepper
hot cooked rice

1. Combine beef, onion and garlic in large skillet. Cook and stir over medium heat until beef is browned, and onion and garlic golden, about 10 minutes.

2. Add beans, tomatoes, chili powder, salt and pepper. Mix gently but well; cover. Simmer about 10 minutes, stirring once or twice.

3. To serve, spoon chili over hot fluffy rice. *Serves 4.*

## HAMBURGER SOUP

4 cups cut-up ripe tomatoes
1 medium onion, quartered
2 cups cut-up carrots
2 cups cut-up celery (with
    leaves)
two 10¾-ounce cans beef
    consommé
2 cups water
2 tablespoons chopped
    parsley
2 or 3 drops hot pepper
    sauce
1½ pounds ground beef
one 7-ounce can tomato
    sauce
2 teaspoons salt
1 teaspoon pepper
½ teaspoon sugar
bay leaf
grated Parmesan cheese
    (optional)

1. In Dutch oven, combine tomatoes, onion, carrots, celery, beef consommé, water, parsley and hot pepper sauce. Bring to boiling point; cover Dutch oven and lower heat. Simmer for 25 minutes.

2. In electric blender or food processor, puree a small amount of mixture from Dutch oven; remove to large bowl. Repeat, pureeing a small amount at a time. Pour pureed mixture back into Dutch oven.

3. Shape ground beef into large patty. Brown patty in medium skillet, 5 minutes per side; break up into chunks. Remove from skillet with slotted spoon.

4. Add ground beef, tomato sauce, salt, pepper, sugar and bay leaf to pureed vegetables in Dutch oven. Simmer 20 minutes, or until bubbly hot. Sprinkle with grated Parmesan cheese, if desired. *Serves 6.*

## VEAL IN WINE

4 veal cutlets or scallops
  (about 1½ pounds)
½ cup flour
1 teaspoon salt
½ teaspoon instant minced
  garlic
¼ teaspoon pepper
½ cup butter or margarine
2 cups sliced mushrooms
⅓ cup white wine

1. Pound veal until very thin. In a large, clean brown paper or plastic bag, mix flour, salt, minced garlic and pepper to make seasoned flour; add veal pieces and shake until veal is well coated with flour.

2. Heat butter or margarine in a medium skillet; add veal and sauté until golden brown. Heap sliced mushrooms over and around veal; pour wine over all.

3. Cover skillet and cook over low heat for 20 minutes. As liquid in skillet cooks down, add a little water, broth or wine to keep veal moist and juicy. *Serves 4.*

## SKILLET VEAL ROULADES

4 veal cutlets or scallops
  (about 1½ pounds)
2 cups packaged stuffing
  mix
2 tablespoons flour
1 teaspoon salt
½ teaspoon pepper
¼ cup butter or margarine
1 cup heavy cream
½ cup dry white wine

1. Pound veal cutlets or scallops until very thin; cut in half to make 8 pieces in all. Prepare stuffing according to label directions.

2. Place the veal on a flat surface. Cover each piece with stuffing; roll up. Mix flour, salt, and pepper in a shallow pan or dish. Place veal rolls in seasoned flour; press in and turn until each roll has a thorough coating. Secure with wooden toothpicks.

3. Shake off excess flour, place veal rolls on waxed paper and chill about 10 to 15 minutes. Heat butter or margarine in a large skillet; add veal rolls and sauté until browned on both sides.

4. Push veal rolls to one side of skillet; add heavy cream and stir well. Stir in wine and heat to a bubble. Push veal rolls back into center of skillet, spooning some pan liquid over each roll.

5. Cover skillet; cook over low heat until the veal rolls are tender, about 20 to 25 minutes. *Serves 4.*

# CREAMY GROUND VEAL

1 tablespoon butter or
   margarine
½ cup chopped onion
1 pound ground veal
one 10¾-ounce can
   condensed cream of
   chicken soup
1 cup sour cream
½ cup grated Parmesan
   cheese
2 tablespoons flour
2 teaspoons salt
saffron- or mustard-
   seasoned rice

1. Melt butter or margarine in large skillet over moderately high heat; add onion and sauté, stirring frequently. Push onion to one side. Shape ground veal into large patty in same skillet; brown 5 minutes per side, then break up into chunks. Lower heat to moderately low.

2. Gradually blend in condensed chicken soup, sour cream, cheese, flour and salt. Cook slowly for 20 minutes or until bubbly hot. Serve over rice. *Serves 4.*

*Note:* To prepare rice, cook 1 cup long-grain rice according to label directions; add 2 or 3 threads saffron or 1 tablespoon mild prepared mustard to cooking liquid.

# VEAL-STUFFED ZUCCHINI

4 medium zucchini
boiling salted water
1 pound ground veal
¼ cup vegetable oil
¼ cup chopped onion
2 cloves garlic, crushed
4 eggs, well beaten
1 cup grated mozzarella
   cheese
2 tablespoons chopped
   parsley
1 teaspoon crumbled thyme
salt and pepper to taste
1 cup buttered fresh bread
   crumbs

1. In large saucepan, cook zucchini in boiling salted water for 10 minutes, or until barely tender. Drain well and cool until easy to handle. Cut each zucchini in half, lengthwise. Scoop out pulp with a spoon and chop. Reserve chopped pulp and shells.

2. Shape ground veal into large patty. Heat oil in large skillet over moderately high heat; brown veal patty, 5 minutes per side. Crumble veal into small pieces and then remove with a slotted spoon to paper towel.

3. Stir onion and garlic into drippings in skillet. Sauté 3 to 5 minutes, or until onion is soft but not browned. Stir in reserved zucchini pulp and cook for 5 minutes. Return veal to skillet. Add beaten eggs, cheese, parsley, thyme, salt and pepper. Stir until well blended.

4. Place reserved zucchini shells in greased 13 x 9 x 2-inch baking dish. Fill with veal mixture. Sprinkle with buttered bread crumbs. Bake at 350° F for 35 minutes, or until topping is golden and zucchini is tender. *Serves 4.*

## FAVORITE VEAL SANDWICHES

4 veal cutlets or scallops
4 slices cooked ham
½ pound mild Cheddar
    cheese
1 egg
2 tablespoons water
¼ cup butter or margarine
¼ cup olive oil

1. Pound veal cutlets or scallops until very thin, about ⅛ inch thick. Cut in half to make 8 pieces in all.

2. Place a slice of ham on each of 4 veal pieces. Cut 4 thin slices from cheese; place on top of ham. Cover cheese with the remaining 4 pieces of veal.

3. Grate remaining piece of cheese into a shallow bowl. In another shallow bowl, beat egg with 2 tablespoons water. Dip veal "sandwiches" first into egg, then into cheese, coating well. Place on waxed paper and let stand in refrigerator 10 minutes.

4. Heat butter or margarine and oil in a large skillet; add veal and sauté over medium heat for about 25 minutes, or until very tender and brown. Use a spatula to carefully turn several times during cooking. When ready to serve, sprinkle any remaining grated cheese over "sandwiches." *Serves 4.*

## PORK CHOPS WITH OREGANO

4 to 6 thin pork chops
    (1 to 1½ pounds)
4 to 6 tablespoons
    vegetable oil
4 to 6 teaspoons crumbled
    oregano

1. Trim off all but ¼ inch of fat from pork chops.

2. In small bowl, combine oil and oregano to form paste. Arrange chops in lightly greased shallow roasting pan or casserole; spread paste on chops. Let stand at room temperature for 30 minutes before cooking.

3. Bake at 375° F for 45 minutes, or until chops are tender when pierced with a fork. Serve with warm applesauce and buttered cabbage wedges. *Serves 4.*

## LEMON PORK CHOPS

4 loin pork chops, 1 inch
    thick
1 large or 2 small lemons
½ cup ketchup
½ cup brown sugar

1. Place chops in shallow baking pan.

2. Thinly slice the lemon or lemons; place 2 slices on each chop. Spread 2 tablespoons ketchup over each chop; sprinkle 2 tablespoons brown sugar over each chop.

3. Bake at 350° F for 45 to 50 minutes until fork tender. *Serves 4.*

# HAM WITH PINEAPPLE AND APRICOTS

¼ cup butter or margarine
one 1-pound ham slice
one 8-ounce can sliced
  pineapple, drained
one 17-ounce can whole
  apricots, drained
3 tablespoons brown sugar
⅛ teaspoon mace or
  nutmeg
¼ cup water or pineapple
  juice

1. Melt butter or margarine in a large skillet. Sauté ham over high heat, about 3 minutes per side. Reduce heat to medium and add pineapple and apricots; spoon hot fat over fruit.

2. Remove ham and fruit from skillet. Add brown sugar and mace or nutmeg to pan juices. Add ¼ cup water or pineapple juice. Stir all together and simmer for a few minutes.

3. Return ham to skillet; cover with the pineapple slices, then top with apricots. Spoon hot pan syrup over fruits and ham. *Serves 4. (Shown on page 52.)*

# HAM AND SPINACH CRESCENTS

one 8-ounce package
  refrigerator crescent rolls
1 egg
1 tablespoon water
one 10-ounce package
  frozen chopped spinach,
  thawed
one 4½-ounce can deviled
  ham
⅓ cup grated Parmesan
  cheese
one 15-ounce jar marinara
  sauce

1. Preheat oven to 375° F. Unroll and separate crescent roll dough into triangles, according to label directions. Beat egg with 1 tablespoon water; brush over triangles.

2. Cook spinach according to label directions. Drain well, then press in strainer to remove all moisture. Mix spinach with ham and cheese.

3. Place a generous spoonful of spinach mixture on each triangle; roll up into a crescent, enclosing filling. Place on greased cookie sheet. Brush again with egg and water.

4. Bake 25 minutes until golden brown. Heat marinara sauce and spoon over crescents before serving. *Serves 4.*

# HAM WAFFLES

2 cups packaged biscuit
  mix
2 tablespoons vegetable oil
1⅓ cups milk
1 egg
one 3-ounce package
  cooked ham, shredded
¼ cup finely chopped apple
1 cup applesauce

1. In a medium bowl, combine biscuit mix, vegetable oil, milk and egg. Beat until smooth.

2. Stir in shredded ham and apple. Use a ladle or measuring cup to pour batter onto center of hot waffle iron. Bake until steaming stops and waffle is done.

3. Use two forks to lift baked waffle from iron. Keep warm while baking remainder of batter. Serve waffles with applesauce. Makes four 9-inch waffles. *Serves 4.*

## CHEESE DOGS WITH BACON

4 long frankfurters
4 teaspoons pickle or hot
  dog relish
4 slices process cheese, cut
  in julienne strips
4 slices bacon
4 frankfurter rolls

1. Preheat broiler. Slit each frankfurter lengthwise. Make a deep slit, but do not cut all the way through. Spread 1 teaspoon relish in each slit.

2. Place strips of cheese in each slit, filling the opening. Wrap each frankfurter with a piece of bacon, spiraling it from one end to the other. Secure with toothpicks.

3. Arrange prepared frankfurters cut side up on broiler pan. Broil about 6 inches from heat until bacon is done and cheese partially melted, 6 to 8 minutes.

4. During last 2 minutes of cooking time, toast frankfurter rolls cut side up under broiler; use to contain Cheese Dogs. *Serves 4.*

## ITALIAN CHICKEN SAUTE

2 whole chicken breasts,
  skinned, boned and cut
  into bite-size pieces
1 teaspoon garlic salt
¼ teaspoon pepper
3 tablespoons butter or
  margarine
one 15½-ounce jar
  spaghetti sauce
1 teaspoon mixed Italian
  herbs
1 cup chopped celery
3 cups hot cooked rice
grated Parmesan cheese

1. Season chicken pieces with garlic salt and pepper.

2. Melt butter or margarine in large skillet over moderately high heat. Add chicken and sauté for 3 minutes, or until lightly browned.

3. Stir in spaghetti sauce and Italian herbs. Lower heat. Cover and simmer about 10 minutes.

4. Add celery; cook 15 minutes longer or until chicken is tender. Serve over rice. Sprinkle with Parmesan cheese. *Serves 4.*

*TimeSaving Tip: Knowing the correct way to skin and bone a chicken breast will save lots of time. Here's the best method: Run fingers between skin and meat; pull skin off smoothly and quickly in one piece (save skin to make chicken broth). Place chicken, meaty side down, on cutting board; press heavily with palms of hands to flatten. Center bone of breast will emerge from flesh; pull out in one piece, loosening flesh from bone with small sharp knife, if necessary. Using same knife, cut between rib bones and flesh; similarly, cut away wishbone at edge of neck. Save bones for chicken broth. Cut breast in half or into bite-size pieces or strips, depending on the recipe.*

## CHICKEN ALMOND STIR-FRY

1½ pounds boned and
    skinned chicken breasts
¼ cup vegetable oil
1 cup blanched almonds
1 tablespoon cornstarch
2 teaspoons sugar
1 teaspoon ginger
⅓ cup sherry
3 tablespoons water
2 tablespoons soy sauce
one 12-ounce package
    frozen Chinese-style
    vegetables, thawed
hot cooked rice

1. Cut chicken breasts into strips, then into small cubes. In a large skillet or wok, heat oil over medium-high heat. Add almonds; cook and stir about 3 minutes until almonds are lightly golden.

2. Reduce heat to medium and add chicken cubes. Cook and stir until chicken turns white.

3. In a small bowl, mix cornstarch, sugar and ginger. Blend in sherry, water and soy sauce to make a smooth mixture.

4. When chicken cubes are fork tender, stir in soy sauce mixture. Continue cooking and stirring until sauce clears and thickens.

5. Add thawed vegetables; stir and cook for 3 or 4 minutes until chicken and vegetables are glazed. Serve over rice. *Serves 4.*

## CHICKEN LIVERS ON RICE

¼ cup chopped onion
2 tablespoons butter or
    margarine
1 pound chicken livers, well
    rinsed
one ¾-ounce package
    hollandaise sauce mix
½ teaspoon dried dill
¼ teaspoon salt
⅔ cup water
one 7¾-ounce can or
    one 6-ounce jar artichoke
    hearts, drained
hot cooked rice

1. Sauté onion in hot butter or margarine in a 12-inch skillet. Pat livers dry on paper towels; add to skillet and brown quickly for 2 or 3 minutes.

2. Remove skillet from heat; push livers to one side. Stir hollandaise sauce mix into drippings in skillet. Mix in dill, salt and ⅔ cup water. Return skillet to very low heat. Stir and cook sauce until bubbly and thickened.

3. Add artichokes and stir all together gently. Cover and simmer 5 minutes or long enough to heat through. Serve over rice. *Serves 4.*

# CHICKEN LIVERS WITH MUSHROOMS

2 slices bacon, cut into
    pieces
1 shallot, finely chopped, or
    2 tablespoons finely
    chopped onion
1 pound chicken livers,
    rinsed and trimmed
1 cup chicken broth
¼ cup sliced mushrooms
2 tablespoons flour
1 teaspoon lemon juice
2 teaspoons cornstarch
1 tablespoon cold water
chopped parsley
hot cooked rice

1. Cook bacon pieces for 5 minutes in large skillet over moderately high heat. Remove from pan with slotted spoon; drain on paper towel.

2. Add chopped shallot or onion to drippings in skillet; sauté for 2 minutes. Add chicken livers and sauté 2 minutes longer.

3. Add chicken broth, mushrooms, flour and lemon juice. Simmer for 5 minutes or until mushrooms are tender.

4. In 1-cup measure, mix cornstarch and water to a smooth paste. Add to skillet. Cook, stirring constantly, until mixture thickens; sprinkle with parsley. Serve on rice. *Serves 4.*

# TURKEY ROLL-UPS

4 slices cooked ham
4 slices mozzarella cheese
4 frozen turkey breast
    slices, thawed
1 tomato, finely chopped
½ teaspoon crumbled sage
⅛ teaspoon pepper
¼ cup butter or margarine,
    melted
⅓ cup dry bread crumbs
2 tablespoons grated
    Parmesan cheese
2 tablespoons chopped
    parsley

1. Make 4 flat packets by placing a slice of ham and a slice of mozzarella cheese on each of 4 thawed turkey slices.

2. Mix finely chopped tomato, sage and pepper. Spread a small amount on each packet. Roll the meat up and secure with toothpicks or small skewers.

3. Place melted butter or margarine in a pie plate. Combine bread crumbs, Parmesan cheese and parsley in another plate or dish. Dip the turkey rolls in melted butter or margarine; roll in bread crumbs.

4. Place turkey rolls in greased pie plate; bake at 350° F for 30 minutes, or until golden brown. *Serves 4.*

## CREAMED TURKEY

4 frozen patty shells (from a
    10-ounce package)
2 cups diced cooked turkey
one 10¾-ounce can
    condensed cream of
    chicken soup
one 10-ounce package
    frozen mixed vegetables,
    thawed
½ cup milk
1 teaspoon finely chopped
    onion
1 teaspoon salt
¼ teaspoon pepper
¼ cup dry white wine
¼ teaspoon fines herbes

1. Bake 4 patty shells according to label directions.

2. In a large saucepan, combine turkey, condensed soup, thawed vegetables, milk, onion, salt and pepper. Mix well; simmer over low heat about 20 minutes, stirring frequently.

3. Stir in wine and fines herbes; heat through about 5 minutes. To serve, fill baked patty shells with creamed turkey and vegetable mixture. *Serves 4.*

*Note:* Return the 2 extra patty shells in package to freezer for later use.

## OPEN-FACE HOT TURKEY SANDWICHES

4 large slices rye bread
butter or margarine
one 8-ounce package sliced
    precooked turkey or
    turkey roll
2 egg whites
¼ teaspoon dry mustard
¼ cup mayonnaise

1. Preheat oven to 400° F. Toast and butter rye bread slices; arrange on baking sheet. Divide turkey slices evenly among bread slices.

2. Beat egg whites with dry mustard until stiff but still moist. Gently fold into mayonnaise.

3. Spoon egg white mixture over turkey; spread evenly. Bake 10 minutes or until topping is slightly puffed and golden. Serve at once. *Serves 4.*

## CURRIED TURKEY SALAD

2 cups diced cooked turkey
¼ cup grated tart apple
½ cup mayonnaise
½ cup unflavored yogurt
2 tablespoons lemon juice
1 teaspoon salt
1 teaspoon curry powder
¼ teaspoon pepper
3 tablespoons finely
    chopped onion
1 tablespoon chopped
    parsley
salad greens

1. In a medium bowl, mix turkey and apple. In a smaller bowl, blend mayonnaise, yogurt, lemon juice, salt, curry powder, pepper, onion and parsley to make a smooth dressing.

2. Add dressing to turkey mixture. Toss until well mixed.

3. Serve on greens with rye toast and cherry tomatoes. *Serves 4.*

## FISH IN DILL SAUCE

½ cup butter or margarine
1 cup finely chopped onion
1 lemon, thinly sliced
1 teaspoon dried dill
1 teaspoon seasoned salt
2 pounds fresh fish fillets, or
  two 16-ounce packages
  frozen fillets, thawed
1 small lemon, cut into
  wedges
parsley

1. Preheat oven to 350° F. Melt butter or margarine in 13 x 9 x 2-inch baking dish. Add onion, lemon slices, dill and seasoned salt; mix well.

2. Place fish in baking dish in one layer. Spoon some of butter mixture from bottom of dish over the fish. Bake 25 to 30 minutes. Garnish with lemon wedges and parsley. *Serves 4.*

## BAKED FISH

one 16-ounce package
  frozen fish fillets, partially
  thawed
½ teaspoon salt
⅛ teaspoon pepper
1 tablespoon butter or
  margarine
one 6-ounce jar hollandaise
  sauce
one 19-ounce can
  asparagus spears
paprika
one 5-ounce package frozen
  French-fried onion rings,
  thawed

1. Preheat oven to 475° F. Arrange fish in 13 x 9 x 2-inch ungreased baking dish, leaving space in center. Sprinkle fish with salt and pepper, dot with butter or margarine. Bake for 15 minutes.

2. Heat hollandaise sauce in top of double boiler over simmering water. Heat asparagus according to label directions; drain well.

3. Remove fish from oven; place drained asparagus spears in center of baking dish and pour hot hollandaise sauce over them. Sprinkle with paprika. Return dish to oven and bake 5 minutes longer.

4. Sprinkle French-fried onion rings over fish. Bake dish an additional 5 minutes. *Serves 4.*

*TimeSaving Tip: When the recipe calls for frozen fish fillets, save time by only partially thawing them before baking. Cooking will take only a minute or two longer than called for with completely thawed fish, and the taste will be superior since fish that is baked while still slightly frozen loses none of its natural juices. All the cooking liquid is retained in the baking pan and can be added to an accompanying sauce for extra flavor (see Baked Fish, above). Whether using packaged fish fillets or whole fish, merely wipe well with paper towels before cooking; rinsing for a prolonged time under cold running water will remove much of the flavor. To clean the cavity of a whole fish, rub with salt and then wipe with damp paper towels. Do not season the cavity with extra salt, but use sprigs of fresh parsley, basil or marjoram to give added taste.*

# FISH AND SPINACH CASSEROLE

one 10-ounce package
  frozen chopped spinach,
  thawed
2 pounds fresh fish fillets, or
  two 16-ounce packages
  frozen fish fillets, thawed
½ cup chopped onion
2 teaspoons lemon juice
½ teaspoon seasoned salt
½ teaspoon pepper
one 11-ounce can
  condensed Cheddar
  cheese soup
½ cup grated Parmesan
  cheese
½ teaspooon oregano
½ cup fresh bread crumbs
1 tablespoon butter or
  margarine, melted

1. Thoroughly drain spinach; spread over bottom of a greased 2-quart shallow casserole.

2. Add fish fillets all in one layer; sprinkle with onion, lemon juice, salt and pepper. Spread condensed Cheddar cheese soup over all.

3. Mix together Parmesan cheese and oregano; sprinkle over soup layer. Top with bread crumbs, tossed with melted butter or margarine. Bake at 350° F for 40 minutes, or until browned and bubbly. *Serves 4.*

# CREAMY PIQUANT BLUEFISH

1½ cups sour cream
½ cup mayonnaise or salad
  dressing
2 tablespoons chopped
  chives
1 tablespoon lemon juice
1 bluefish, cleaned and
  dressed (about 2 pounds)
salt and pepper to taste

1. Preheat oven to 350° F. In medium bowl, combine sour cream, mayonnaise or salad dressing, chives and lemon juice. Stir to mix well.

2. Place bluefish in ungreased shallow oval casserole. Sprinkle with salt and pepper. Cover with sour cream mixture. Bake 30 minutes, or until fish flakes easily. *Serves 4.*

Welsh Rarebit with Mushrooms (page 27)

Italian Pasta Potpourri (page 29)

Asparagus and Beef Stir-Fry (page 33)

Ham with Pineapple and Apricots (page 42)

## DOUBLE QUICK CRAB

one 6½-ounce can
　crabmeat, drained
one 10¾-ounce can
　condensed cream of
　shrimp soup
one 3-ounce package cream
　cheese, softened
1 tablespoon sherry
hot cooked rice

1. Flake crabmeat into the top of a double boiler, discarding all pieces of cartilage. Add condensed shrimp soup and softened cream cheese.

2. Heat through over simmering water; stir in sherry. Serve crab over hot fluffy rice. *Serves 4.*

## CREAMY CRAB CASSEROLE

two 6-ounce packages
　frozen crabmeat or
　crabmeat and shrimp
　combination, thawed
3 hard-cooked eggs,
　chopped
1 cup heavy cream
1 cup mayonnaise
⅓ cup sour cream
1 tablespoon chopped
　parsley
1 teaspoon grated onion
½ teaspoon salt
¼ teaspoon pepper
¼ cup butter or margarine,
　melted
½ cup fine seasoned bread
　crumbs or crushed
　stuffing mix
hot cooked rice

1. Drain and remove cartilage from thawed crabmeat or crabmeat and shrimp combination. Then, mix together with hard-cooked eggs and heavy cream in a large bowl.

2. Fold in mayonnaise and sour cream. Add parsley, onion, salt and pepper. Turn mixture into a 2-quart casserole.

3. Mix melted butter or margarine with bread crumbs; sprinkle over top of casserole. Bake at 350° F for 25 to 30 minutes. Serve over rice. *Serves 4.*

## TUNA ON RICE

¼ cup butter or margarine
¼ cup flour
¼ cup milk
½ cup heavy cream
¼ cup sherry
2 tablespoons lemon juice
2 tablespoons
   Worcestershire sauce
1 teaspoon seasoned salt
¼ teaspoon dry mustard
one 7-ounce can tuna,
   drained and flaked
3 hard-cooked eggs,
   chopped
¼ cup grated Parmesan
   cheese
¼ cup fresh bread crumbs
1 tablespoon butter or
   margarine, melted
hot cooked rice

1.  Melt butter or margarine in a large saucepan; stir in flour. Cook and stir for 2 or 3 minutes until smooth and bubbly. Stir in milk until smooth; blend in heavy cream.

2.  Cook and stir over low heat until thick and smooth. Stir in sherry, lemon juice, Worcestershire sauce, salt and dry mustard. Cook and stir for 2 or 3 minutes longer. Stir in tuna and eggs.

3.  Turn tuna mixture into a greased 1½-quart casserole. Combine cheese, bread crumbs and melted butter or margarine; sprinkle over top. Bake at 375° F for 25 to 30 minutes, or until browned and bubbly. Serve over hot fluffy rice. *Serves 4.*

## TUNA SALAD ON A ROLL

one 7-ounce can tuna,
   drained and flaked
½ cup chopped celery
½ cup mayonnaise
1 tablespoon chopped onion
1 teaspoon seasoned salt
⅛ teaspoon pepper
4 large French rolls or Italian
   sandwich rolls
butter or margarine
1 large tomato, cut in
   4 slices
4 slices process cheese

1.  In a medium bowl, mix tuna, celery, mayonnaise, onion, salt and pepper.

2.  Split, toast and butter rolls. Divide tuna filling among bottom halves of the rolls; top each with a tomato slice and a cheese slice.

3.  Broil until cheese bubbles. Cover with toasted top halves of rolls. *Serves 4.*

## TUNA NOODLE CASSEROLE

one 8-ounce package fine
  egg noodles
boiling water
one 10¾-ounce can
  condensed cream of
  celery soup
½ cup light cream
⅓ cup mayonnaise or salad
  dressing
¼ cup chopped onion
1 teaspoon salt
2 cups cubed sharp
  Cheddar cheese
one 7-ounce can tuna,
  drained and flaked
1 cup crumbs (bread,
  cracker or potato chips)

1. Cook noodles in boiling water according to label directions; drain and set aside.

2. In electric blender, process condensed celery soup, light cream, mayonnaise or salad dressing, onion and salt at high speed until smooth. Add cheese, piece by piece, and process until thoroughly blended.

3. Pour pureed mixture into a greased 2-quart casserole. Add tuna and the cooked noodles. Toss to mix well. Top with crumbs. Bake at 375° F for 35 minutes, or until bubbly. *Serves 4.*

## EGGS BENEDICT

about 4 cups water
1 teaspoon vinegar
½ teaspoon salt
8 eggs
4 English muffins
butter or margarine
one 12-ounce can luncheon
  meat, cut in 8 slices
one 3-ounce jar hollandaise
  sauce

1. Fill a medium skillet two thirds full with water. Add vinegar and salt; bring to boiling point. Reduce heat to just under a boil. Slip in eggs one at a time and poach until eggs are done.

2. Meanwhile, split, toast and butter the muffins. Sauté slices of luncheon meat in small skillet. Warm hollandaise sauce in double boiler.

3. Place a slice of luncheon meat on each muffin. Remove poached eggs from water, one at a time, using a buttered skimmer or perforated spoon.

4. Place eggs on slices of luncheon meat; top with hollandaise sauce. *Serves 4.*

# PABLO'S TORTILLA

⅔ cup vegetable oil or
 olive oil
1 cup thin onion rings
4 cups peeled and very
 thinly sliced potatoes
1 teaspoon salt
7 eggs
¼ cup chopped parsley

1. Heat oil in large skillet or omelet pan over medium heat. Add onion rings, potatoes and salt. Spread in skillet and cook until potatoes are tender and mixture is slightly browned, about 10 to 15 minutes. Use a spatula to turn mixture as it browns.

2. Remove potatoes and onions from skillet with slotted spoon; set aside. Remove skillet from heat; pour off and reserve excess oil. In a large bowl, beat eggs. Stir in drained, cooked potatoes and onions.

3. Wipe out skillet and add 1 tablespoon reserved oil; heat. Pour egg mixture into skillet; cook and stir over medium heat, lifting at edges and allowing egg to run under.

4. When egg mixture begins to set, loosen tortilla around edges and shake to loosen from bottom of skillet. Cover skillet with 12-inch platter and turn both over together so that tortilla is positioned on the platter, cooked side up. Immediately slide tortilla back into skillet and cook 3 minutes longer, or until tortilla is golden and cooked on both sides. Shake skillet constantly to keep tortilla loose in skillet.

5. Slide tortilla onto large platter; sprinkle with chopped parsley. Cut into wedges to serve. *Serves 4 generously.*

*TimeSaving Tip:* *The onions and potatoes for the tortilla can be sliced quickly in a food processor or on a vegetable slicer. The latter is called a "mandolin" by professional chefs, and is an oblong wooden board containing steel knives, both plain and serrated, which can be adjusted for thin or thick slices.*

*Use a heavy iron skillet or omelet pan to make a crisp tortilla. The fastest way to season the skillet (so the tortilla will not stick) is to add salt to a ½-inch depth, then heat for 10 minutes over low heat. Wipe clean with oily paper towels before using; also wipe clean with oily paper towels after use. This is particularly important for omelet pans.*

## MR. ROBERTSON'S QUICHE

½ cup finely chopped onion
½ cup dry white wine
4 eggs
1 cup milk
1 cup heavy cream
1 teaspoon salt
¼ teaspoon white pepper
pinch of nutmeg
¾ pound Gruyère cheese,
  grated
½ pound Swiss cheese,
  grated
one 9- or 10-inch frozen
  prepared pie shell

1. Preheat oven to 400° F. In a small saucepan, combine onion and wine; bring to boiling point. Reduce heat and simmer for 2 or 3 minutes. Cool to room temperature.

2. In a large bowl, beat eggs, milk and heavy cream together until foamy. Add salt, white pepper and nutmeg. Stir in cooled onion and wine mixture.

3. Mix the grated Gruyère and Swiss cheese together and sprinkle over bottom of prepared pie shell in an even layer.

4. Pour the egg and cream mixture over the grated cheese. Bake 25 minutes or until center is set. *Serves 4 generously.*

## MAKE-YOUR-OWN PIZZA

1 pound ground beef
one 12-ounce package bulk
  sausage meat
2 refrigerator or frozen pizza
  shells, unbaked
one 15-ounce can seasoned
  tomato sauce
one 6-ounce can tomato
  paste
2 teaspoons oregano
one 4½-ounce jar sliced
  mushrooms, drained
½ cup diced pepperoni
½ cup diced salami
½ cup chopped provolone
  cheese
2 cups shredded mozzarella
  cheese

1. Preheat oven to 400° F. Brown ground beef in medium skillet; remove from skillet with slotted spoon and set aside. Cook sausage in same skillet, crumbling with a fork as it cooks. Remove from skillet, drain on paper towels and set aside.

2. Place each pizza shell on a cookie sheet. Mix together the tomato sauce and tomato paste in a 1-quart measure; divide between the 2 pizza shells. Sprinkle the oregano over the tomato mixture.

3. Spread reserved ground beef over 1 pizza shell; spread reserved sausage over the other shell. Divide mushrooms between the 2 shells.

4. In a medium bowl, toss together pepperoni, salami and provolone cheese. Divide mixture between the pizza shells and spread out evenly. Sprinkle the shredded mozzarella cheese over all.

5. Bake for 10 to 12 minutes until cheese bubbles and edges brown. *Serves 4 generously.*

## MANICOTTI PARMESAN

one 32-ounce package
  frozen stuffed manicotti
one 15-ounce can tomato
  sauce
1 teaspoon crumbled
  oregano
½ cup grated Parmesan
  cheese

1. Place frozen manicotti in a greased 13 x 9 x 2-inch baking pan. Pour tomato sauce over manicotti; sprinkle with oregano. Sprinkle Parmesan cheese on top.

2. Bake at 350° F for 45 minutes, or until sauce is bubbly and manicotti is heated through. *Serves 4.*

## COUNTRY CLUB SQUASH

8 small zucchini
1 teaspoon salt
1 teaspoon pepper
2 tablespoons butter or
  margarine
1 chicken bouillon cube,
  crushed
1 tablespoon grated onion
1 egg, beaten
1 cup sour cream
½ cup grated sharp cheese
½ cup fine dry bread
  crumbs
paprika

1. Trim zucchini; cut into pieces. Cook in boiling water to cover until fork tender. Drain very well, then mash.

2. To mashed zucchini, add salt, pepper, butter or margarine, crushed bouillon cube and onion. Mix very well.

3. Stir in beaten egg and sour cream. Turn mixture into a greased 1-quart casserole. Mix cheese, bread crumbs and paprika; spread over mixture in casserole. Bake at 350° F for about 35 minutes until lightly browned and bubbly. *Serves 4.*

*TimeSaving Tip: To save time and energy, no preheating instructions have been given (except where necessary, such as for breads, egg dishes, pastry, etc.). Five minutes have been added to the baking time of those dishes that are placed in a cold oven.*

# SIXTY-MINUTE MENUS

CHAPTER | THREE

**W**hen the occasion calls for something special but time is short, don't panic. You can count on any of the 20-plus menus in this chapter to move you smoothly and quickly from basic ingredients to a delectable, gourmet dinner in 60 minutes—or less.

Try the Veal Sauté Menu, for example: hot Crab-Stuffed Mushrooms for starters, followed by sautéed veal cutlets served in a delicate white wine and cream sauce, Spinach Pie and a refreshing endive-lychee salad, all topped by a light dessert of Vanilla Ice Cream with Apricot Sauce. The work plan with the menu will take you through every step in getting this dinner on the table fast.

To avoid last-minute hassles, keep a few special ingredients on hand; they'll make even the most impromptu party memorable:

- Cans of pâté and escargots. An elegant first course sets the tone for the entire dinner.
- Frozen filet mignon steaks, veal scallops, lamb chops or shrimp for an extra special main course. Thaw these in the refrigerator, if possible.
- Frozen asparagus and artichoke hearts, canned artichoke bottoms and jars of celery hearts. One very special vegetable lends an extra touch of class.
- Gourmet staples such as imported olive oil, chutney, capers, anchovies, good wine vinegar, fresh shallots and garlic, whole black and green peppercorns, and a fine French mustard.
- Classic dessert makings such as fruits bottled in liqueur, chestnuts in syrup, black cherries, frozen strawberries or raspberries and a container of top-quality ice cream.

With these tips and the menus in this chapter, a party-special dinner couldn't be easier—or more delicious.

# STEAK AU POIVRE MENU

TRI-COLOR SALAD

**STEAK AU POIVRE**
WITH SAVORY SAUCE

FRENCH FRIES

**SPINACH-TOMATO
CASSEROLE**

**WARM LEMON SOUFFLE**

Serves 4.

**WORK PLAN:** *Prepare **Spinach-Tomato Casserole**. Place 1 large Boston lettuce leaf on each of 4 salad plates; top each with 3 thin slices tomato and some celery root; chill. Serve with mustard mayonnaise as a first course. Cook one 32-ounce polybag frozen French fries according to label directions. Prepare **Warm Lemon Soufflé**. Make **Steak au Poivre**. Just before steaks are done, melt ¼ cup butter or margarine with 1 tablespoon lemon juice and 1 teaspoon Worcestershire sauce in small saucepan; serve this savory sauce with steaks.*

## SPINACH-TOMATO CASSEROLE

two 10-ounce packages
    frozen chopped spinach,
    thawed and very well
    drained
one 6-ounce can mushroom
    slices in butter sauce
one 14½-ounce can sliced
    baby tomatoes, drained
1 tablespoon butter or
    margarine
1 tablespoon flour
½ cup milk
1 teaspoon instant minced
    onion
¼ teaspoon dry mustard
½ cup grated sharp Cheddar
    cheese
1 tablespoon grated
    Parmesan cheese

1. In a 1-quart casserole or soufflé dish, place well-drained spinach. Top with mushrooms, then with tomatoes.

2. Melt butter or margarine in small saucepan. Stir in flour. Slowly add milk, then minced onion and dry mustard. Cook, stirring constantly, until sauce thickens and bubbles, about 3 minutes. Stir in grated Cheddar and Parmesan cheese. Pour sauce over vegetables in casserole.

3. Bake at 350° F for 50 minutes, or until casserole is bubbly hot.

## WARM LEMON SOUFFLE

¾ cup superfine sugar
5 eggs, separated
1 teaspoon grated lemon
  rind
¼ cup fresh lemon juice
¼ teaspoon cream of tartar
1 cup heavy cream
¼ cup sifted confectioners'
  sugar
1 teaspoon vanilla extract

1. Grease a 1½-quart soufflé dish; sprinkle with 1 table-spoon of the superfine sugar. Make an aluminum foil collar and tie it around the dish, greasing the inside of the collar. Preheat oven to 350° F.

2. With electric mixer at high speed, beat egg yolks in medium bowl until light. Slowly add remaining superfine sugar, beating until smooth and creamy. Add lemon rind and juice. Thoroughly wash and dry the beaters.

3. With electric mixer at high speed, beat egg whites and cream of tartar in a clean, medium bowl until stiff. Gently fold into egg yolk mixture. Pour into prepared soufflé dish. Place in roasting pan on oven rack. Fill pan with warm water to depth of 1 inch.

4. Bake 35 minutes, or until puffy and golden on top.

5. Meanwhile, using electric mixer at high speed, beat heavy cream in small bowl, slowly adding confectioners' sugar and vanilla extract. Beat just until beaters leave soft tracks on the surface of the cream, *no more.*

6. Serve soufflé immediately, passing cream to spoon on top of each serving.

## STEAK AU POIVRE

1½ to 2 tablespoons whole
  peppercorns
4 filet mignon steaks, 1 inch
  thick
1 tablespoon salted butter
  or margarine
¼ cup brandy

1. Place peppercorns on a board between two sheets of waxed paper. Crush with the bottom of a skillet or rolling pin. Press crushed peppercorns into steaks on both sides. If necessary, use palms of hands or bottom of skillet to get peppercorn pieces to adhere.

2. Melt butter or margarine in large heavy skillet until very hot. Add steaks and brown on one side; turn steaks and reduce heat. Cook slowly, about 2 to 6 minutes per side.

3. In small saucepan, warm the brandy. Pour over steaks, stand back and ignite with long kitchen match. When flames subside, remove steaks to warm platter and serve.

# FILET MIGNON MENU

**STUFFED MUSHROOMS**

FILET MIGNON,
BEARNAISE SAUCE

**GARLICKED
CHERRY TOMATOES**

FETTUCCINE VERDE

CHEESECAKE
WITH GREEN GRAPES

Serves 4.

*WORK PLAN: Begin by preparing dessert: Refrigerate one 16-ounce store-bought cheesecake on serving platter; simmer 1 cup seedless green grape halves with 2 tablespoons each honey, sweet sherry and chopped crystallized ginger for 5 minutes. Cool grape topping in freezer, then add to cheesecake; garnish with mint leaves. Next, prepare* **Stuffed Mushrooms.** *Prepare* **Garlicked Cherry Tomatoes** *and* **Fettuccine Verde.** *Meanwhile, make filet mignon with Béarnaise sauce. For the sauce, heat 1 cup mayonnaise with 2 tablespoons each grated onion or shallots and tarragon vinegar in top of double boiler over simmering water. For the filets, heat 2 tablespoons olive oil in large skillet over medium heat; sauté 1 clove garlic, slivered, until brown. Discard garlic. Sauté 1-inch-thick steaks, 2 to 6 minutes per side, sprinkling cooked sides with salt and pepper. Serve on a large heated platter, surrounded by the cherry tomatoes. (Menu shown on page 85.)*

# STUFFED MUSHROOMS

20 large mushrooms
vegetable oil
1 slice Swiss cheese
chopped fresh tarragon or
    parsley
20 bay scallops (about 1
    pound)
¼ cup butter or margarine,
    melted and browned
chopped parsley

1. Remove stems from mushrooms and reserve for another recipe. Lightly brush outside of caps with oil, using pastry brush.

2. Cut cheese into tiny pieces, about ¼ x ¼ inch in size, or small enough to fit inside mushroom caps. Fill caps with cheese, then sprinkle with chopped tarragon or parsley.

3. Fit scallops into each cap, in upright position to resemble stems. Divide stuffed mushrooms between individual au gratin dishes or place in a shallow baking pan. Brush liberally with browned butter.

4. Bake at 375° F for 20 minutes, or until mushrooms are tender, scallops are cooked, and both are hot and bubbly. Garnish with chopped parsley.

## GARLICKED CHERRY TOMATOES

1 pint cherry tomatoes
½ cup butter or margarine
2 cloves garlic, crushed
salt and pepper to taste
watercress (optional)

1. Wash and remove stems from tomatoes. Pat dry.

2. Melt butter or margarine with crushed garlic in large skillet over medium heat. Cook garlic, stirring often, about 5 minutes. Remove garlic with a slotted spoon.

3. Add tomatoes and sauté, turning them very gently with large spoon, for 5 minutes, or until heated through but not mushy. Add salt and pepper and garnish with watercress, if you wish.

## FETTUCCINE VERDE

6 quarts water
1 tablespoon salt
½ cup butter or margarine
2 cloves garlic, finely
   chopped
one 16-ounce package
   green fettuccine
one 10-ounce package
   frozen peas, thawed
½ cup freshly grated
   Parmesan cheese
⅓ cup shredded cooked
   ham
6 mushrooms, sliced and
   sautéed in butter

1. Bring water and salt to boiling point in large saucepan.

2. Melt butter or margarine in skillet over low heat. Add garlic and cook slowly until soft, but not brown.

3. Add fettuccine to boiling salted water. Cook according to label directions until tender, about 8 minutes. Drain immediately in colander and return to saucepan.

4. Add the melted butter and garlic to saucepan, along with the thawed peas, cheese, ham and sautéed mushrooms. Toss over very low heat until well blended and heated through. Serve immediately. *Serves 6.*

# STEAK DIANE MENU

**ARTICHOKE BOTTOMS
WITH CAVIAR**

**STEAK DIANE**

STUFFED ONIONS

**ZUCCHINI BAKE**

ENDIVE AND
WATERCRESS SALAD

**CHERRIES JUBILEE**

Serves 4.

**WORK PLAN:** *Prepare* **Artichoke Bottoms with Caviar,** *then* **Zucchini Bake.** *Prepare Stuffed Onions: Peel 16 small white onions; cut off top of each and remove one thin outer layer to form a cup-like shell. (Reserve rest of onions for later use; place in large plastic bag, seal and refrigerate.) Place onion shells in large roasting pan and fill with mixture of ½ pound softened liverwurst blended with ¼ cup brandy, ¼ cup chopped parsley and 2 cloves garlic, crushed. Pour 1 cup dry white wine into pan; cover and cook beside Zucchini Bake for 20 to 25 minutes. While vegetables bake, prepare salad: In large bowl, combine 2 cups each bite-size pieces endive and watercress sprigs; chill. (Just before serving, toss with mixture of ⅓ cup peanut oil, 2 tablespoons tarragon vinegar and 1 tablespoon Dijon-style mustard.) Assemble ingredients for* **Cherries Jubilee,** *to be prepared at the table for dessert. Prepare* **Steak Diane.**

# ARTICHOKE BOTTOMS WITH CAVIAR

one 3-ounce package cream
  cheese, softened
2 tablespoons sour cream
2 teaspoons grated onion
½ teaspoon seasoned salt
2 drops hot pepper sauce
one 7¾-ounce can
  artichoke bottoms,
  drained
one 3½-ounce jar red or
  black caviar
lettuce

1. In a small bowl, thoroughly blend softened cream cheese, sour cream, grated onion, seasoned salt and hot pepper sauce.

2. Place drained artichoke bottoms on a flat dish. Fill each one with a spoonful of cream cheese mixture; top with a generous amount of caviar. Chill.

3. Arrange on lettuce leaves and serve as first course.

## ZUCCHINI BAKE

3 cups chopped zucchini
⅓ cup chopped onion
⅓ cup sliced water
  chestnuts
⅓ cup sour cream
1 tablespoon chopped
  parsley
½ teaspoon salt
⅛ teaspoon pepper
⅓ cup packaged bread
  crumbs
3 tablespoons butter or
  margarine, softened
3 tablespoons grated
  Parmesan cheese

1. In a greased 1-quart casserole, mix chopped zucchini, onion, water chestnuts, sour cream, parsley, salt and pepper. Mixture will look dry, but do not add any liquid.

2. In a small bowl, use a fork to thoroughly mix bread crumbs, butter or margarine, and cheese. Sprinkle evenly over zucchini mixture.

3. Bake casserole at 350° F for 30 to 35 minutes.

## CHERRIES JUBILEE

one 29-ounce can pitted
  dark sweet cherries
½ cup currant jelly
½ cup brandy, warmed
1½ pints vanilla ice cream

1. Drain cherries, reserving ½ cup of the juice. In a chafing dish, mix cherries, the reserved ½ cup cherry juice and the currant jelly. Heat to a bubble, stirring to melt jelly.

2. Pour warmed brandy over cherries; ignite at once.

3. When flames subside, ladle cherries over scoops of vanilla ice cream.

## STEAK DIANE

4 rib-eye or tenderloin
  steaks, about ½ inch
  thick
black pepper
2 tablespoons olive oil
¼ cup butter or margarine
½ cup chopped green
  onions
½ cup chopped parsley
1 tablespoon lemon juice
2 teaspoons Dijon-style
  mustard
1 tablespoon cornstarch
one 10½-ounce can beef
  broth
¼ cup port
¼ cup brandy

1. Trim steaks and pound to ¼-inch thickness. Sprinkle with freshly ground black pepper; brush lightly with olive oil.

2. Heat 1 tablespoon of the olive oil and 2 tablespoons of the butter or margarine in a skillet or frying pan. When fat is very hot, quickly sauté steaks about ½ minute per side. Remove steaks and keep warm.

3. Add remaining oil and butter to skillet. Stir in green onions, parsley and lemon juice; cook about 1 minute.

4. In a 4-cup measure, mix mustard, cornstarch and beef broth until blended and smooth. Add to skillet, stirring continuously. Stir over moderately low heat until mixture begins to bubble and thicken.

5. Stir in port and brandy; cook 1 minute longer. Return steaks to skillet and heat through. Serve with sauce.

# SIRLOIN STEAK MENU

SIRLOIN STEAK

HASH-BROWN POTATOES

**TOMATOES STUFFED
WITH SPINACH**

CELERY-WALNUT
BIBB SALAD

**STRAWBERRIES AND
PINEAPPLE CHANTILLY**

Serves 4.

*WORK PLAN: Prepare **Strawberries and Pineapple Chantilly**. For salad, arrange 1 small head Bibb lettuce, cut in quarters, on each of 4 salad plates; top each with ½ cup thin slices of celery and 2 tablespoons chopped walnuts. (Pass oil and vinegar at serving time.) Prepare **Tomatoes Stuffed with Spinach**. Prepare hash browns by frying 4 cups coarsely grated potatoes in large skillet with ½ cup butter or margarine, 1½ teaspoons salt and ½ teaspoon pepper; turn potatoes frequently. Meanwhile, prepare steak: Heat ¼ cup olive oil in large skillet; sauté one 1½- to 2-pound sirloin steak (1 inch thick) for 5 to 9 minutes per side, sprinkling each cooked side with 1 teaspoon seasoned salt and ¼ teaspoon pepper.*

# STRAWBERRIES AND PINEAPPLE CHANTILLY

1 small fresh pineapple
2 pints strawberries, hulled
  and halved
2 tablespoons sugar
3 tablespoons orange
  liqueur
1 cup heavy cream
3 tablespoons sifted
  confectioners' sugar
1 teaspoon vanilla extract

1. Quarter, core and cut fruit away from the shell of pineapple; cube the fruit.

2. In large bowl, combine pineapple cubes and halved strawberries. Sprinkle with 2 tablespoons sugar and toss gently; sprinkle with orange liqueur. Cover with plastic wrap and chill. (If you are in a hurry, place fruit in freezer; it must be served very cold.)

3. At serving time, whip the heavy cream until semi-thick, slowly adding 3 tablespoons confectioners' sugar and the vanilla extract. Beat just until beaters leave soft tracks on the surface of the cream, *no more.*

4. Divide fruit among 4 glass bowls; top with cream. Serve extra cream alongside.

## TOMATOES STUFFED WITH SPINACH

4 large firm tomatoes
salt
one 16-ounce package
  frozen creamed spinach,
  thawed
½ cup dry bread crumbs
1 tablespoon butter or
  margarine

1. Cut tops off tomatoes. Scoop out insides; turn tomato shells upside down to drain.

2. Place right side up in a 13 x 9 x 2-inch baking pán. Sprinkle insides with salt. Spoon in uncooked thawed spinach until tops are slightly mounded. Sprinkle with bread crumbs and dot with butter or margarine.

3. Bake at 350° F for 25 minutes, or until tomatoes are tender, but not mushy.

# FLANK STEAK MENU

**STUFFED FLANK STEAK**
BROWNED ONIONS
PARMESAN SPINACH
CUCUMBER SALAD
WITH TOMATO WEDGES
**RASPBERRY SOUFFLE,**
STRAWBERRY SAUCE

Serves 4.

*WORK PLAN: Prepare **Stuffed Flank Steak.** For salad, combine 2 cups each thin cucumber slices and tomato wedges and ½ cup Greek olives; chill. (Just before serving, toss with dressing made from ½ cup buttermilk and ¼ cup each chopped fresh parsley and chives.) Next, prepare Browned Onions: Melt 3 tablespoons butter or margarine in large skillet over medium heat. Add one 16-ounce package frozen small onions, thawed; sauté, turning to brown all sides. Add ¼ cup red wine; cover and simmer until wine evaporates. Surround cooked flank steak with browned onions. Meanwhile, prepare spinach: Wash and drain 1 pound spinach leaves; cook, covered, over low heat until wilted. Toss with 2 tablespoons each grated Parmesan cheese and butter or margarine, 1 teaspoon salt, and ¼ teaspoon each nutmeg and pepper; keep warm. Prepare **Raspberry Soufflé** and pop it in the oven as you sit down to dinner. Serve with strawberry sauce made by heating together 1 cup strawberry jelly and 1 cup sliced fresh strawberries.*

## STUFFED FLANK STEAK

one flank steak
  (about 2 pounds)
olive or vegetable oil
⅓ cup butter or margarine
¼ cup chopped onion
1 stalk celery, chopped
1 cup packaged herb
  stuffing mix (from an
  8-ounce package)
one 8-ounce can mushroom
  stems and pieces, drained
1 teaspoon crumbled thyme
¼ teaspoon salt
1 cup thickly sliced
  mushrooms
2 tablespoons butter or
  margarine
2 tablespoons lemon juice
chopped parsley

1. Have butcher cut a full pocket in flank steak. Brush both sides of steak with oil. Place steak in small roasting pan. Preheat oven to 350° F.

2. Melt the ⅓ cup butter or margarine in large skillet. Add onion and celery and sauté until transparent. Add stuffing mix, mushroom stems and pieces, thyme and salt. Mix until well blended.

3. Stuff flank steak pocket with mixture. Skewer closed and bake for 40 minutes. Place on heated serving platter and keep warm.

4. In small skillet, lightly sauté the 1 cup sliced mushrooms in the 2 tablespoons butter or margarine and the lemon juice. Pour mushrooms and pan juices over steak and sprinkle with chopped parsley.

## RASPBERRY SOUFFLE

one 12-ounce package
  frozen raspberries, thawed
3 tablespoons sugar
3 tablespoons cornstarch
2 egg yolks
6 egg whites
⅓ cup sugar

1. Preheat oven to 350° F. Puree the raspberries. Place in saucepan and blend in the 3 tablespoons of sugar and the cornstarch. Heat to boiling, stirring constantly. Off heat, quickly beat in the 2 egg yolks, stirring rapidly until mixture is cool.

2. In large bowl, beat the 6 egg whites until stiff (be sure the beaters are thoroughly clean and dry). Gradually beat in the ⅓ cup sugar. Fold the egg whites into the raspberry mixture; spoon into greased 1-quart soufflé dish.

3. Bake in oven for 30 minutes. Serve immediately.

# SCANDINAVIAN MEATBALLS MENU

HERRING SALAD

**SCANDINAVIAN MEATBALLS**

BROWN-WHITE RICE

GREEN BEANS AND WATER CHESTNUTS

**BAKED APPLES**

Serves 4.

**WORK PLAN:** *Prepare **Baked Apples** and **Scandinavian Meatballs**. In the meantime, prepare salad: Drain two 8-ounce jars herring in wine sauce; divide among 4 lettuce-lined salad plates. Top each serving with 2 tablespoons sour cream and 1 tablespoon chopped parsley, and garnish with lemon wedges; chill until serving time. Cook one 6-ounce package long-grain and brown rice mix according to label directions; keep warm. Cook one 20-ounce polybag frozen cut green beans according to label directions; drain and add one 7-ounce can water chestnuts, drained and sliced, and 2 tablespoons butter or margarine. Heat until water chestnuts are hot.*

## BAKED APPLES

4 large baking apples
4 pitted dates
½ cup sliced almonds
¼ cup brown sugar
¼ cup butter or margarine
1 cup white wine
½ cup water
2 tablespoons apricot preserves

1. Select Rome Beauties, Stayman or Winesap apples. Core and remove 1-inch strip of skin around top of each apple. Arrange in baking pan.

2. Stuff each apple with a date and sprinkle with 2 tablespoons almonds and 1 tablespoon brown sugar. Dot with 1 tablespoon butter or margarine.

3. Mix wine and water; pour around apples. Cover with foil and bake at 350° F for 35 minutes. Baste 2 or 3 times with liquid in pan.

4. When ready to serve, stir preserves into liquid in pan, heat and spoon over apples.

# SCANDINAVIAN MEATBALLS

**2 tablespoons butter or margarine**
**1 cup chopped mushrooms**
**½ cup chopped onion**
**1 slice bread, crusts trimmed**
**¼ cup cold water**
**½ pound ground beef**
**¼ pound ground veal**
**¼ pound ground pork**
**1 egg**
**1 tablespoon chopped parsley**
**1 tablespoon lemon juice**
**½ teaspoon grated lemon rind**
**½ teaspoon salt**
**¼ teaspoon pepper**
**⅛ teaspoon nutmeg**
**about 1 cup flour**
**one 10½-ounce can beef broth**
**2 tablespoons capers**
**1 tablespoon cornstarch**
**¼ cup water**

1. Melt butter or margarine in a large heavy skillet. Add mushrooms and onion; sauté.

2. Soak bread in cold water; squeeze dry. In a large bowl, mix bread, ground beef, veal, pork and egg. Blend in parsley, lemon juice and rind, salt, pepper and nutmeg.

3. Use a large kitchen spoon to mix sautéed mushrooms and onion into meat mixture. Shape mixture into balls (about the size of apricots). Roll the meatballs in flour, then brown on all sides in skillet, adding more butter or margarine if necessary.

4. Remove any excess fat from skillet and add beef broth. Simmer for 20 minutes. Add capers.

5. Blend cornstarch and water until smooth. Stir into pan liquid. Simmer and stir until gravy is slightly thickened.

*TimeSaving Tip:* *A quick trick for shaping meatballs is to roll them between wet hands before rolling them lightly in flour for a crisp crust after browning. If rolled into tiny ½-inch balls and sautéed as directed, they need to simmer for only 10 minutes—perfect as an appetizer or at cocktail time as an hors d'oeuvre. Other good-to-know tricks: For added lightness, soak bread in club soda before adding to meatballs. For speed, use a meat baster to siphon off excess fat from skillet, before adding beef broth. And for extra flavor, use ¼ cup red wine instead of water to blend with the cornstarch.*

*Use whatever ground meat you have on hand; any combination can be used in the recipe on this page. If preferred, the entire pound of meat can be ground beef. Remember, ground chuck has more fat and therefore more flavor; ground round has less fat so the main flavor of the mixture will come from the ground pork.*

# HAM-ASPARAGUS MENU

HAM-ASPARAGUS
MORNAY

CAULIFLOWER
ALMONDINE

WILTED SPINACH

CLUB ROLLS

**APPLE FOAM**

Serves 4.

**WORK PLAN:** *Prepare* **Apple Foam.** *Then, wash 1 small head cauliflower, remove all leaves and simmer cauliflower until tender in 1 inch boiling salted water for about 25 to 30 minutes; drain. Heat ½ cup butter or margarine and ¼ cup slivered almonds in small skillet until butter is brown and almonds are golden; pour over cauliflower just before serving. Prepare* **Ham-Asparagus Mornay,** *heating some club rolls alongside the casserole. To prepare spinach, wash, drain and remove coarse leaves from 1½ pounds fresh spinach; cook in covered saucepan until wilted. Drain and toss with 2 tablespoons butter or margarine, 2 tablespoons lemon juice and 1 teaspoon salt.*

## APPLE FOAM

2 large tart apples, peeled
   and cored
1 tablespoon sugar
1 teaspoon lemon juice
⅛ teaspoon nutmeg
2 egg whites
1 cup heavy cream
sugar or honey
cinnamon

1. Grate apples into a medium bowl. Stir in 1 tablespoon sugar, the lemon juice and nutmeg.

2. Beat egg whites until stiff but not dry; fold into apple mixture. Spoon into a glass serving bowl.

3. Whip the heavy cream and sweeten to taste with sugar or honey. Pile on top of apple mixture; dust cinnamon over all. Chill.

## HAM-ASPARAGUS MORNAY

one 15-ounce can white
   asparagus
4 thin slices cooked ham
2 tablespoons butter or
   margarine
2 tablespoons flour
1 cup milk
½ teaspoon salt
⅛ teaspoon white pepper
⅛ teaspoon nutmeg
pinch of cayenne pepper
⅓ cup grated Parmesan
   cheese
1 egg yolk
1 tablespoon water

1. Place a cluster of 4 asparagus spears at one end of each slice of ham; roll up, making 4 separate bundles. Place ham rolls in 1-quart casserole.

2. Melt butter or margarine in a small saucepan over medium heat. Stir in flour. Cook and stir until mixture is golden; add milk. Cook and stir until thickened and smooth, about 2 minutes.

3. Stir in salt, white pepper, nutmeg and cayenne pepper. Add ¼ cup of the Parmesan cheese; mix well. Stir in egg yolk beaten with 1 tablespoon water. Reduce heat to low and continue to cook 1 minute longer. Sauce should be very smooth.

4. Pour sauce over ham rolls; dust top with remaining grated cheese. Bake at 375° F for 20 minutes until top is lightly browned.

# VEAL SAUTE MENU

CRAB-STUFFED
MUSHROOMS
**VEAL SAUTE**
**SPINACH PIE**
ENDIVE-LYCHEE SALAD
**VANILLA ICE CREAM
WITH APRICOT SAUCE**

Serves 4.

*WORK PLAN: Prepare **Spinach Pie**. Prepare **Vanilla Ice Cream with Apricot Sauce**. To make salad, arrange spear-like leaves from 2 small endives on 4 salad plates; top with drained lychees from one 11-ounce can; chill. (Just before serving, top with dressing made by blending 1/2 cup unflavored yogurt, 2 tablespoons each honey and lemon juice and 1/2 teaspoon curry powder.) Prepare **Veal Sauté**. Make **Crab-Stuffed Mushrooms** and bake beside Spinach Pie for final 25 minutes of pie's cooking time.*

## SPINACH PIE

2 eggs
one 16-ounce package
   frozen creamed spinach,
   thawed
one 8-inch frozen prepared
   pie shell, thawed
nutmeg

1. Preheat oven to 350° F.

2. In medium bowl, beat eggs. Stir in thawed spinach until well blended. Pour into prepared pie shell. Sprinkle nutmeg on top.

3. Bake 40 minutes, or until knife inserted in center comes out clean and crust is golden brown.

## VANILLA ICE CREAM WITH APRICOT SAUCE

1½ pints vanilla ice cream
one 8¾-ounce can unpeeled
   apricots, drained and
   pitted
2 tablespoons superfine
   sugar
1 tablespoon lemon juice

1. Scoop vanilla ice cream into 4 dessert dishes and return to freezer.

2. Place apricots, sugar and lemon juice in container of electric blender. Cover and process on high speed until smooth. When ready to serve, divide sauce among dishes of ice cream. Makes about 1 cup sauce.

## VEAL SAUTE

1½ pounds veal cutlets or
 scallops
5 tablespoons butter or
 margarine
¼ cup vegetable oil
1 tablespoon finely chopped
 shallots
⅓ cup dry white wine
1 cup heavy cream
⅛ teaspoon pepper

1. Pound veal to ¼-inch thickness. Cut into 2 x ¼-inch strips.

2. Heat 2 tablespoons of the butter or margarine and half of the oil in large skillet over medium heat until foamy. Add half the veal strips and sauté for 2 minutes. Remove veal to a heated plate and keep warm. Repeat with 2 more tablespoons of the butter or margarine, and the remaining oil and veal; remove veal to heated plate.

3. Melt the remaining tablespoon of butter or margarine in skillet. Add shallots and cook until soft, not brown. Add wine and bring to boiling point. Add heavy cream, pepper and any juices that have accumulated from veal. Bring to boiling point. Boil 10 minutes, stirring constantly, until sauce is reduced by half.

4. Return veal to skillet. Cook over low heat until veal is heated through. Serve immediately.

## CRAB-STUFFED MUSHROOMS

1 pound fresh mushrooms
 (about 24)
vegetable oil
one 6½-ounce can
 crabmeat, drained and
 flaked
3 tablespoons bread
 crumbs
3 tablespoons grated
 Gruyère cheese
2 tablespoons mayonnaise
 or salad dressing
1 tablespoon lemon juice
⅛ teaspoon pepper
parsley sprigs

1. Remove stems from mushrooms and save for another use. Wipe caps with damp paper towels. Brush outside of each mushroom cap with oil, using pastry brush.

2. In small bowl, combine crabmeat (cartilage removed), bread crumbs, cheese, mayonnaise or salad dressing, lemon juice and pepper until well blended. Stuff mushrooms with crab mixture. Place in 4 individual baking dishes or in a 13 x 9 x 2-inch baking pan.

3. Bake at 350° F for 20 to 25 minutes, or until mushrooms are tender and filling is bubbly hot. Garnish with parsley sprigs.

# VEAL PAPRIKA MENU

CONSOMME WITH
SESAME BREADSTICKS
**VEAL PAPRIKA**
**RISOTTO**
LIMA BEANS AND DILL
**ZABAGLIONE
OVER FRUIT**

Serves 4.

**WORK PLAN:** *Prepare* **Veal Paprika** *and* **Risotto.** *Cook one 20-ounce polybag frozen baby limas according to label directions; drain, and toss with 2 tablespoons each butter or margarine and chopped fresh dill. Next, prepare* **Zabaglione over Fruit;** *chill fruit in stemmed glasses while keeping custard warm. Heat two 10-ounce cans chicken consommé with 1/4 cup dry sherry; serve with sesame breadsticks as a first course.*

# VEAL PAPRIKA

1 tablespoon olive oil
1 tablespoon butter or
  margarine
1½ pounds veal shoulder,
  cut into ¾-inch cubes
2 cups chopped
  mushrooms
1½ cups chopped onions
1 tablespoon flour
1 tablespoon paprika
½ teaspoon crumbled
  thyme
½ teaspoon crumbled
  rosemary
½ teaspoon salt
⅛ teaspoon pepper
2 cups chicken broth or
  water
1 cup Madeira wine or sweet
  sherry
½ cup sour cream

1. Heat oil and butter or margarine in a large skillet. Sauté veal, mushrooms and onions. Stir in flour and cook until golden.

2. Add paprika, thyme, rosemary, salt and pepper. Stir in broth or water and Madeira wine or sweet sherry.

3. Simmer 35 to 40 minutes, stirring occasionally. Just before serving, stir in sour cream. Heat, but do *not* boil.

## RISOTTO

½ cup butter or margarine
1 cup long-grain rice
½ cup chopped onion
1 cup dry white wine
1 cup chicken broth
1 teaspoon salt
¼ teaspoon pepper

1. In medium skillet, melt butter or margarine; stir in rice and onion. Cook and stir over medium heat until rice is golden and onion translucent.

2. Stir in wine, chicken broth, salt and pepper. Mix well and bring to boiling point.

3. Reduce heat to low, cover and simmer 25 to 30 minutes.

## ZABAGLIONE OVER FRUIT

3 egg yolks
1 cup white wine or Marsala
2 tablespoons sugar
⅛ teaspoon ginger
fresh fruit, diced, and/or
    berries, rinsed
sliced almonds (optional)

1. In the top part of a double boiler, beat egg yolks with white wine or Marsala, sugar and ginger. Place over simmering water in bottom section of double boiler.

2. Use a wire whisk to beat egg mixture until frothy and thickened.

3. Serve while warm over diced fresh fruit and/or berries in stemmed glasses. Sprinkle with sliced almonds, if desired.

*TimeSaving Tip: Sesame breadsticks are available in supermarkets, but if you have a moment, why not make up a batch at home? Store them in an airtight container to have on hand to serve with menus that are prepared in a hurry. You can make breadsticks in several ways, depending on available time and ingredients:*

*Simple Breadsticks: Trim crusts from 4 slices of white bread (½ inch thick); brush both sides with melted butter or margarine. Cut lengthwise into ½-inch strips, then toss in plastic bag with 2 tablespoons sesame seeds. Bake on cookie sheet at 400° F for 10 to 15 minutes or until crisp. Makes 32.*

*Easy Breadsticks: Cut refrigerator rolls (from an 8-ounce package) in half. Roll each into a 4-inch strip; brush with a little beaten egg white and water. Sprinkle with sesame seeds and bake at 400° F for 10 to 15 minutes or until crisp. Makes 20.*

# VEAL SCALLOPS MENU

MUSHROOM SOUP
**VEAL SCALLOPS
WITH CHICKEN LIVERS**
RICE
ASPARAGUS
WITH BREAD CRUMBS
**APPLES IN SNOW**

Serves 4.

*WORK PLAN: Prepare soup: Combine two 10½-ounce cans beef broth and ½ cup each dry sherry and finely chopped mushrooms; heat through and keep warm. Prepare* **Apples in Snow.** *Next, make* **Veal Scallops with Chicken Livers;** *keep warm. Cook 1½ cups long-grain rice according to label directions. In large skillet, cook 1½ pounds washed and trimmed asparagus in ½ inch of boiling salted water until just tender (or prepare two 10-ounce packages frozen asparagus spears according to label directions); drain, and toss with 2 tablespoons each butter or margarine and lemon juice, and sprinkle with ½ cup fresh bread crumbs.*

## APPLES IN SNOW

4 Golden Delicious apples, peeled and cored
4 heaping tablespoons Nesselrode, butterscotch morsels, nuts or chopped dates
½ cup or more dry white vermouth
2 pieces lemon rind
4 teaspoons sugar
4 teaspoons butter or margarine, melted
4 egg whites
⅛ teaspoon cream of tartar
¼ cup sugar
¼ teaspoon vanilla extract
4 rounds pound cake, toasted
2 teaspoons seedless raspberry jelly

1. Stuff apples with filling of your choice. Place in greased shallow baking pan. Pour vermouth into pan to a depth of ½ inch. Toss in lemon rind. Sprinkle the 4 teaspoons of sugar, then drizzle the 4 teaspoons of butter or margarine over apples.

2. Bake at 350° F for 40 minutes, or until apples are tender; baste every 10 minutes. Remove from oven and increase heat to 500° F.

3. Using electric mixer at high speed, beat egg whites with cream of tartar in small bowl until foamy white and double in volume. Gradually beat in ¼ cup sugar, 1 tablespoon at a time. Beat well after each addition, and continue beating until mixture is glossy and forms stiff peaks. Fold in vanilla extract.

4. Spread rounds of toasted pound cake with jelly. Place on cookie sheet or in individual baking dishes. Top each with an apple. With rubber spatula, cover apple and cake with meringue, leaving cored section uncovered. Place in upper third of oven.

5. Bake 2 minutes, or until meringue is tinged with gold. Serve with sauce apples were cooked in, removing lemon rind and adding sugar, if necessary.

# VEAL SCALLOPS WITH CHICKEN LIVERS

¼ cup butter or margarine
¼ pound chicken livers, rinsed and patted dry
½ cup chopped green onions
¼ cup chopped prosciutto ham
2 tablespoons chopped parsley
⅛ teaspoon crumbled sage
⅛ teaspoon salt
8 veal scallops, pounded to ¼-inch thickness
½ cup flour
3 tablespoons vegetable oil
1 cup chicken broth
½ cup Madeira wine
hot cooked rice

1. Melt 2 tablespoons of the butter or margarine in small skillet over moderate heat. Add chicken livers and sauté until brown on all sides and cooked through. Remove from skillet and chop. Place in small bowl.

2. Add green onions and prosciutto to skillet. Sauté 2 minutes. Add to chicken livers along with parsley, sage and salt; mix until well blended.

3. Divide liver stuffing into 8 portions; place a portion in middle of each veal scallop. Roll up and tie with string to secure. Dredge in flour on waxed paper.

4. Melt remaining 2 tablespoons butter or margarine and the oil in a large skillet. Add veal rolls and brown on all sides. Remove from skillet and pour off fat. Deglaze skillet with chicken broth and the wine, stirring up browned bits from bottom. Bring to boiling point; boil 1 minute.

5. Return veal to skillet. Cover and reduce heat. Simmer 15 minutes, or until veal is tender. Remove veal from skillet to a warm serving platter and remove string. If necessary, boil down liquid in skillet to ½ cup. Pour over veal and serve surrounded with rice.

*TimeSaving Tip: Pound veal scallops between two sheets of foil or plastic wrap (not waxed paper). Use flat side of wooden mallet only, or wooden rolling pin. Thin slices of veal shoulder or even veal breast can be substituted for the veal scallops; just tenderize the veal with meat tenderizer before pounding. A good time-saving and budget-saving substitute for the prosciutto ham in this recipe is semi-soft salami. Genoa salami is the best and much easier to find than prosciutto.*

*Quickly make fresh bread crumbs for the cooked asparagus by whirling day-old bread slices, cubed, in an electric blender. No blender? Just lightly grate the bread slices against the coarsest side of a grater.*

*Use fruit in season for dessert. Pears are ideal and can be substituted for the apples in Apples in Snow. Fresh peach halves, peeled and pitted, would also be a good alternative, as would thick slices of fresh pineapple. Thick rings from a tiny cantaloupe could be placed directly on the toasted rounds of pound cake; fill the center with stuffing, cover with meringue, and bake a few minutes, as directed.*

# LAMB CHOP MENU

**VEGETABLE COMPASS**
GRILLED LAMB CHOPS
MINTED CARROTS
POTATO CHIPS
**BLUEBERRY BETTY** AND
VANILLA ICE CREAM

Serves 6.

*WORK PLAN:* Start by preparing **Blueberry Betty,** then **Vegetable Compass.** While the dessert is cooling, broil six 1½-inch-thick lamb chops, 6 inches from heat, 5 to 9 minutes per side. Brush frequently with mixture of ¼ cup each honey, soy sauce and sherry, and 1½ teaspoons each basil and rosemary. Meanwhile, cook 2 pounds carrots, cut into julienne strips, in boiling salted water for about 5 to 7 minutes, until crisp-tender; drain, and toss with ¼ cup each butter or margarine and chopped mint. Wrap potato chips from one 16-ounce bag in foil; just before serving, heat for a few minutes in the oven. During dinner, leave 1 pint vanilla ice cream out of freezer to soften as a topping for Blueberry Betty.

## BLUEBERRY BETTY

1 pint fresh blueberries,
   rinsed and picked over, or
   two 10-ounce packages
   frozen blueberries, thawed
1 teaspoon lemon juice
½ teaspoon cinnamon
¾ cup flour
¾ cup sugar
⅓ cup butter or margarine

1. Preheat oven to 350° F. Combine berries with lemon juice and cinnamon in a 1-quart baking dish.

2. In small bowl, combine flour and sugar. Cut in butter or margarine to form crumb topping. Sprinkle over berries in baking dish.

3. Bake 30 minutes, or until topping is golden and berries are tender. Cool briefly; serve warm, spooning into small bowls.

*Note:* This is a very versatile recipe. Apples or peaches can be substituted for the blueberries. Temperature can be adjusted from 250° F to 450° F to accommodate other dishes. It also holds well for several hours in a warm oven.

# VEGETABLE COMPASS

1 large head unblemished
  cauliflower
1 cup mayonnaise or salad
  dressing
¼ cup Dijon-style mustard
1½ teaspoons dried dill
one 4½-ounce can small
  shrimp, chilled
one 10-ounce package
  frozen peas, thawed
½ cup chopped onion
½ cup sour cream
1 tablespoon lemon juice
⅛ teaspoon salt and pepper
leafy lettuce
1 bunch green onions,
  trimmed
6 tomatoes, sliced
bottled Italian dressing
chopped parsley

1. Remove green leaves from cauliflower. Place whole cauliflower in collapsible steamer in a large saucepan. Steam 15 to 20 minutes, or until crisp-tender. Immediately submerge in a bowl of ice water for a few minutes to stop cooking process. Drain and finish cooling in refrigerator until serving time. (If necessary, quick-chill in freezer.)

2. In small bowl, combine mayonnaise or salad dressing, mustard and ½ teaspoon of the dill. Cover with plastic wrap and chill until serving time.

3. Drain shrimp and rinse in a strainer under cold running water. In medium bowl, combine shrimp, peas, onion, sour cream, lemon juice, ½ teaspoon of the dill, and the salt and pepper. Cover with plastic wrap and chill until serving time.

4. Line 12-inch serving platter with leafy lettuce. Place chilled cauliflower in center. Arrange green onions around cauliflower in spoke fashion, so that platter is divided into four sections. Place small mounds of shrimp-pea mixture and the sliced tomatoes in alternate sections. Drizzle tomatoes with Italian dressing and sprinkle with chopped parsley. Pour chilled mustard mayonnaise over top of cauliflower; sprinkle with the remaining ½ teaspoon of dill. Serve with metal salad spoon and fork for easier serving.

*TimeSaving Tip: The focus of this meal is the appetizer, which takes the longest amount of time to prepare. To speed the cooking process of the cauliflower, insert a knife several times into the thickest part of the main stem. Quick-chill the cooked cauliflower in the freezer for 30 minutes (use a timer to avoid over-chilling). The mayonnaise dressing and shrimp can be quick-chilled in the freezer, too. Peas can be thawed quickly in a microwave oven or placed in a strainer under cold running water for 3 minutes; remember to drain them well. After all the ingredients have been prepared and assembled, it will take 10 minutes at most to arrange the Vegetable Compass.*

*Depending on the season, other selections of fish and vegetables can be arranged around the cauliflower. Instead of shrimp, try clams, mussels, oysters or baby sardines. For vegetables, try sliced zucchini or yellow summer squash, cucumbers, thinly sliced radishes, button mushrooms, and green and red pepper strips.*

# SKEWERED LAMB MENU

**ESCARGOTS IN
MUSHROOM CAPS**

FRENCH BREAD

**SKEWERED LAMB**

TABBOULEH

**GREEN BEANS
IN LEMON SAUCE**

**PUFF PANCAKE FLAMBE**

Serves 6.

*WORK PLAN: While marinating lamb cubes for **Skewered Lamb**, prepare tabbouleh by tossing wheat pilaf
(bulgur wheat) from two 16-ounce cans with ¹/₂ cup
olive oil, ¹/₄ cup lemon juice, 2 tablespoons chopped
mint, 2 teaspoons grated lemon rind and ¹/₂ teaspoon
pepper. Mound in center of 6 lettuce-lined salad plates;
surround with tomato wedges and chill. Prepare **Escargots in Mushroom Caps.** Wrap a loaf of French bread in
foil and heat alongside (and use to soak up the snail
butter). Keep escargots and bread warm until serving
time. Prepare **Green Beans in Lemon Sauce;** keep warm.
Broil the skewered lamb cubes, then prepare **Puff Pancake Flambé,** to be baked during dinner.*

## SKEWERED LAMB

½ cup lemon juice
½ cup olive or vegetable oil
2 tablespoons chopped
  fresh mint, or 1 teaspoon
  crumbled dried mint
1 clove garlic, crushed
½ teaspoon salt
¼ teaspoon pepper
2½ pounds boneless leg of
  lamb, cut into 1½-inch
  cubes

1. In 2-cup measure, mix lemon juice, oil, mint, garlic, salt
and pepper until well blended. Pour over lamb cubes in a
glass dish. Cover with plastic wrap and marinate for about
45 minutes.

2. Preheat broiler. Remove lamb from marinade, reserving
marinade; divide lamb cubes among 6 long skewers.

3. Broil 4 inches from heat, turning frequently and brush-
ing with reserved marinade. Broil for about 12 minutes, or
until lamb is brown on the outside, but still slightly pink on
the inside.

## ESCARGOTS IN MUSHROOM CAPS

18 very large mushrooms
vegetable oil
18 snails (4½-ounce can)
½ cup butter or margarine,
  softened
2 tablespoons finely
  chopped parsley
2 cloves garlic, crushed

1. Remove stems from mushrooms. Rub outside of caps
with oil; tuck snails into caps.

2. In small bowl, mix together the softened butter or margarine, parsley and garlic. Seal each snail with garlic butter,
spreading it with a knife. As mushroom caps are buttered,
place stuffed side up in two 13 x 9 x 2-inch baking pans.
Spread any extra garlic butter over snails.

3. Bake at 350° F for 20 minutes, or until mushrooms and
snails are cooked. Serve hot with French bread.

## GREEN BEANS IN LEMON SAUCE

1½ pounds fresh green
   beans, or one 20-ounce
   polybag frozen green
   beans
¼ cup butter or margarine
¾ cup light cream
1 egg
3 tablespoons freshly grated
   Parmesan cheese
salt and pepper to taste
¼ teaspoon nutmeg
2 tablespoons lemon juice

1. In large saucepan, cook beans in boiling salted water until crisp-tender. Drain well and return to saucepan.

2. Add butter or margarine and all but 2 tablespoons of the cream. Cook over medium heat for 1 minute.

3. In 1-cup measure, beat egg. Stir in cheese, the remaining 2 tablespoons cream, salt, pepper and nutmeg. Add lemon juice. Beat, then add lemon sauce to beans. Cook, stirring gently, for 2 to 3 minutes, or until sauce has thickened and beans are well coated. Do *not* boil.

## PUFF PANCAKE FLAMBE

½ cup flour
½ cup milk
2 eggs, slightly beaten
¼ cup butter or margarine
2 tablespoons
   confectioners' sugar
2 tablespoons orange juice
¼ cup orange liqueur

1. Preheat oven to 425° F. In medium bowl, combine flour, milk and eggs. Batter will be slightly lumpy.

2. Melt butter or margarine in 12-inch skillet with heatproof handle. When very hot, pour batter into skillet and place in the oven.

3. Bake 15 to 20 minutes. Do not open oven door during cooking time.

4. Remove from oven. Sift confectioners' sugar over top. Return to oven 1 minute. Remove from oven and sprinkle with orange juice.

5. Meanwhile, heat orange liqueur in a small saucepan, but *do not boil.* At the table, pour warm orange liqueur over the pancake; carefully ignite. Spoon mounds of pancake onto dessert plates as flames subside.

# PORK CHOP MENU

CHESTNUT SOUP
**PORK CHOPS VERONIKA**
BAKED RICE
BRUSSELS SPROUTS
**BRIE EN CROUTE**
WITH COMICE PEARS

Serves 4.

**WORK PLAN:** *First, make* **Chestnut Soup;** *keep warm. Prepare* **Pork Chops Veronika.** *Chill some Comice pears and prepare* **Brie en Croute.** *At the same time, bake 1½ cups long-grain rice according to label directions. For vegetables, trim base and tough leaves from 1½ pounds Brussels sprouts; cut deep cross in base of each. Simmer sprouts, covered, in 1 inch of boiling salted water for 7 to 10 minutes or until tender (or prepare two 10-ounce packages of frozen Brussels sprouts according to label directions); drain.*

## CHESTNUT SOUP

one 15-ounce can chestnut puree (1½ cups)
one 10½-ounce can beef broth
1 cup milk
1 cup heavy cream
½ cup dry sherry
1 to 2 tablespoons tomato paste

1. Use a wire whisk to blend together chestnut puree, beef broth, milk and cream in large saucepan.

2. Stir over medium heat about 8 to 10 minutes until mixture is heated through.

3. Blend in sherry and tomato paste with whisk. Heat through and serve hot.

## PORK CHOPS VERONIKA

1 teaspoon salt
½ teaspoon sage
¼ teaspoon pepper
4 rib or top loin pork chops, about 1½ inches thick
1 cup dry white wine
1 small lemon, thinly sliced
2 tablespoons drained capers
2 tablespoons sour cream

1. Mix salt, sage and pepper. Sprinkle mixture on both sides of pork chops; use the back of a teaspoon to rub and press seasoning into chops.

2. Trim a little fat from edge of each chop; melt fat in large skillet over medium heat. Brown chops, 2 minutes per side; pour off surplus fat.

3. Add wine and lemon slices to skillet; simmer over low heat for 30 minutes, until chops are fork tender.

4. Stir in the capers and sour cream. Heat through, but do *not* boil.

## BRIE EN CROUTE

one 4½-ounce wedge Brie
2 frozen patty shells, thawed (from a 10-ounce package)
1 egg white

1. Preheat oven to 400° F. Keep Brie refrigerated until ready to use; it should be fairly firm while being prepared for oven.

2. Use a rolling pin to press together and flatten the thawed patty shells; roll out into square big enough to cover the cheese.

3. Place cheese in center of dough and wrap so cheese is completely covered. Brush edges with a little water and press firmly to seal in cheese. Brush with egg white beaten to a froth. Place in pie plate and bake for 25 minutes.

# GRIOTTES MENU

**GRIOTTES WITH TI-MALISE SAUCE**

YAMS

GREEN SALAD WITH MANDARIN ORANGES

**BAKED BANANAS**

Serves 4.

*WORK PLAN: To make salad, combine 4 cups leafy salad greens, one 11-ounce can mandarin oranges, drained, and ½ cup thin red onion rings in large bowl; chill. (Just before serving, toss with dressing of ½ cup unflavored yogurt, 2 tablespoons lemon juice and 1 tablespoon prepared mild mustard.) Prepare* **Griottes with Ti-Malise Sauce.** *While Griottes are simmering, peel and cut 1½ pounds yams into ½-inch slices. Cook yams in 1 inch of boiling salted water until tender, about 10 minutes; drain, and toss with 2 tablespoons each butter or margarine and brown sugar and ½ teaspoon cinnamon. Prepare* **Baked Bananas.**

## GRIOTTES

¼ cup vegetable oil
2 pounds lean pork loin, cut into 2-inch cubes
1 cup finely chopped onion
¼ cup finely chopped green onions (white part only)
1 cup fresh orange juice
½ cup fresh lime juice
½ teaspoon salt
½ teaspoon pepper
½ teaspoon crumbled thyme
Ti-Malise Sauce (page 84)

1. Heat oil in a heavy skillet over medium heat. Add pork cubes and brown on all sides. Stir in onion and green onions. Cook 1 minute, or until slightly wilted.

2. Stir in orange juice, lime juice, salt, pepper and thyme. Bring to boiling point. Reduce heat and cover; simmer 30 minutes. (Meanwhile, begin marinating the chopped onion for Ti-Malise Sauce.)

3. Uncover skillet and increase heat to medium. Cook pork cubes 10 minutes longer, stirring constantly, until sauce becomes a syrupy glaze. Serve with Ti-Malise Sauce, passed separately.

## Ti-Malise Sauce

1 cup chopped onion
½ cup fresh lime juice
1 tablespoon butter or
   margarine
1 teaspoon finely chopped
   fresh chili pepper
½ teaspoon finely chopped
   garlic
1 teaspoon salt

1. In small bowl, marinate onion in lime juice for 25 minutes. Drain, reserving juice.

2. Melt butter or margarine in a heavy skillet. Add onion and cook until soft, not brown. Add chili pepper and garlic.

3. Cover and cook over low heat for 10 minutes, or until chili pepper is tender. Remove skillet from heat. Stir in reserved lime juice and the salt. Serve at room temperature. *Makes about 1½ cups.*

## BAKED BANANAS

one 8-ounce package cream
   cheese, softened
⅓ cup dark brown sugar,
   firmly packed
1 teaspoon cinnamon
4 large firm bananas, peeled
3 tablespoons butter or
   margarine
⅓ cup heavy cream

1. In small bowl, combine cream cheese, brown sugar and ¾ teaspoon of the cinnamon until well blended and fluffy.

2. Cut bananas in half, lengthwise. Set aside a shallow baking dish, large enough to hold the 8 banana halves. Melt butter or margarine in a large skillet. Add banana halves and brown on both sides. As they brown, put them into baking dish.

3. Cover bananas with cream cheese mixture. Pour heavy cream over all.

4. Bake at 350° F for 15 minutes, or until bubbly and brown. Remove from oven and sprinkle the remaining ¼ teaspoon cinnamon on top. Serve immediately.

Filet Mignon Menu (pages 62 and 63)

Coulibiac Menu (pages 90 and 91)

Cook-Ahead Day Three (pages 114 to 121)

# PORK TENDERLOIN MENU

**PORK TENDERLOIN
GUATEMALA**

**QUICK CORN PUDDING**

COOKED CABBAGE
IN SOUR CREAM

GRAPEFRUIT SALAD

**PEAR BETTY**
WITH HARD SAUCE

Serves 4.

**WORK PLAN:** *Prepare **Pork Tenderloin Guatemala,** then **Quick Corn Pudding,** baking pudding alongside pork. Make salad by arranging peeled sections from 2 large grapefruit alternately with slices from 1 ripe avocado on romaine leaves in shallow serving bowl. Sprinkle with seeds from half a pomegranate; chill, and serve with a vinaigrette or creamy salad dressing. Next, prepare **Pear Betty.** Then, shred 1 small head cabbage and cook in boiling salted water until crisp-tender, about 2 to 4 minutes. Drain, and toss in heated serving bowl with 1 cup sour cream and 1 tablespoon chopped chives.*

## PORK TENDERLOIN GUATEMALA

1½ pound whole pork
  tenderloin
1 teaspoon salt
¼ teaspoon pepper
½ cup tomato juice
½ cup soy sauce
⅓ cup honey
1 clove garlic, crushed
¼ teaspoon ginger

1. Place pork in shallow roasting pan. Sprinkle with salt and pepper. Bake at 350° F for 35 minutes.

2. Meanwhile, combine tomato juice, soy sauce, honey, garlic and ginger in medium saucepan. Simmer for 15 minutes, or until flavors are blended.

3. Brush pork with tomato mixture. Bake 30 minutes longer, basting with tomato mixture every 10 minutes. Slice and serve with remaining tomato mixture.

## QUICK CORN PUDDING

one 16½-ounce can cream-
  style corn
½ cup light cream
2 eggs
½ teaspoon salt
¼ cup fresh bread crumbs

1. Preheat oven to 350° F. Pour corn into a greased 1-quart casserole or baking dish. Stir in light cream, eggs and salt; mix until well blended.

2. Sprinkle bread crumbs over corn.

3. Bake 45 minutes, or until bubbly and firm.

## PEAR BETTY

1¼ cups soft bread crumbs
3 cups sliced pared pears
½ cup brown sugar, packed
½ cup chopped pecans
¼ cup dark rum
½ teaspoon cinnamon
½ teaspoon nutmeg
3 tablespoons butter
hard sauce

1. In a greased 1-quart casserole, place half of the bread crumbs. Top with pears, brown sugar, pecans, rum, cinnamon and nutmeg. Sprinkle remaining bread crumbs over the top and dot with butter.

2. Bake at 350° F for about 35 to 45 minutes, or until pears are tender and crumbs are golden. Serve with hard sauce.

# COULIBIAC MENU

WATERCRESS SOUP
**COULIBIAC**
CUCUMBER SALAD
**COFFEE MOUSSE**

Serves 4.

**WORK PLAN:** *Make* **Coffee Mousse.** *Prepare* **Coulibiac.** *While Coulibiac bakes, prepare soup and salad. Heat two 10½-ounce cans chicken broth, 1 cup chopped watercress leaves, packed, and 2 tablespoons lemon juice; keep warm. Toss together 4 cups sliced cucumbers and ½ cup garlic dressing. Divide among 4 salad plates; sprinkle each portion with ¼ cup chopped parsley. (Menu shown on page 88.)*

# COFFEE MOUSSE

¾ cup sugar
1 envelope unflavored gelatin
1 cup water
2 tablespoons freeze-dried coffee
2 egg whites
½ cup heavy cream

1. In small saucepan, combine sugar and gelatin; stir in 1 cup water. Heat over low heat just until gelatin is dissolved.

2. Stir in freeze-dried coffee; chill quickly in freezer until semi-set, about 15 minutes. Meanwhile, stiffly beat the egg whites, then the heavy cream.

3. When coffee mixture is just semi-set, beat with electric mixer at high speed until frothy; fold in the beaten egg whites and the beaten heavy cream. Divide between 4 parfait glasses and chill.

**TimeSaving Tip:** *To prepare dough for a perfect crisp-crusted Coulibiac in no time at all, there is one trick to know: Make sure the patty shells are thawed but still icy cold to the touch. Dough that is at room temperature will be buttery and difficult to roll and shape with precision. Carefully seal the sides and ends of the dough to contain the filling; dampen edges of dough with water, or better yet, brush thoroughly with egg white before pinching together firmly. If desired, trim the dough into a precise rectangle before sealing; use the dough scraps to form a decoration on top after the Coulibiac has been placed seam side down on the cookie sheet. The egg yolk glaze will ensure a golden-brown shiny crust.*

*Here's a recipe for the garlic dressing called for in the Cucumber Salad (above): ⅓ cup olive or vegetable oil, 2 tablespoons wine vinegar, 2 cloves garlic (finely chopped), 1 teaspoon each salt, sugar and dry mustard, and ¼ teaspoon pepper. For a stronger garlic flavor, crush garlic and salt together to form a paste before beating into dressing.*

# COULIBIAC

1 tablespoon dried
  mushrooms
½ cup water
¼ cup butter or margarine
½ cup chopped green
  onions
½ cup chopped parsley
¼ cup Madeira wine
½ teaspoon white pepper
⅛ teaspoon ground
  cinnamon
⅛ teaspoon ground nutmeg
⅛ teaspoon ground cloves
⅛ teaspoon ground allspice
one 16-ounce can pink
  salmon, drained and
  flaked
2 tablespoons flour
1 cup milk
one 10-ounce package
  frozen patty shells,
  thawed
1 cup cooked rice
2 hard-cooked eggs, sliced
1 raw egg
1 teaspoon milk
lemon wedges

1. Preheat oven to 425° F. Soak dried mushrooms in ½ cup water for 5 minutes. Melt 2 tablespoons of the butter or margarine in large skillet over medium heat. Add green onions and parsley and sauté until limp. Stir in wine, mushrooms (and the water in which they were soaked), white pepper, cinnamon, nutmeg, cloves and allspice. Bring to boiling point. Lower heat and simmer for 7 minutes. Carefully stir in flaked salmon (discarding bones). Cook 1 minute. Remove from heat and cool.

2. Melt remaining 2 tablespoons butter or margarine in small saucepan. Stir in the flour. Slowly pour in 1 cup milk, stirring with wire whisk to prevent lumps. Cook, stirring all the time, until mixture thickens and bubbles, about 3 minutes. Remove from heat.

3. Arrange patty shells on a floured board in two rows so that they are all touching. Roll and shape dough into a 10 x 14-inch rectangle.

4. Leaving a 3-inch border all around, spread half of cooked rice over dough, then half of white sauce, half of salmon mixture and 1 sliced egg. Repeat with remaining rice, white sauce, salmon mixture and the second sliced egg. Fold dough in from sides and pinch together at the center. Fold in ends and pinch. Brush seams with a little water to help seal dough. Slide a greased cookie sheet under filled dough and turn dough seam side down. Make small hole or slits in top.

5. Beat the raw egg with 1 teaspoon milk. Brush mixture over dough.

6. Bake 25 minutes, or until crust is golden brown. Serve hot or cold, with lemon wedges on the side. *Serves 6.*

# SALMON SOUFFLE MENU

**SALMON SOUFFLE
WITH LEMON SAUCE**

**CUCUMBER AND PEAS**

CORN

VEGETABLE SALAD

BLUEBERRIES
WITH CAKE FINGERS

Serves 4.

**WORK PLAN:** *Begin by making salad: In large bowl, combine 2 cups each bite-size pieces of fresh spinach and fresh bean sprouts, and 1 cup each julienne strips zucchini and tomato wedges; chill. (Just before serving, toss with ½ cup herb and spice dressing.) For dessert, divide 1 pint fresh blueberries (or two 10-ounce packages frozen blueberries, thawed) among 4 parfait glasses; chill. To serve, top each with 2 tablespoons sour cream and a sprinkling of maple or brown sugar; serve with toasted pound cake or angel food cake fingers. Make* **Salmon Soufflé with Lemon Sauce.** *Prepare* **Cucumber and Peas.** *Cook 4 cups fresh-cut kernel corn in ½ cup boiling salted water until tender (or prepare one 32-ounce polybag frozen whole kernel corn according to label directions); drain, and toss with 2 tablespoons butter or margarine and 1 tablespoon sugar.*

# SALMON SOUFFLE

**3 tablespoons butter or
   margarine**
**⅓ cup chopped onion**
**¼ cup chopped green
   pepper**
**3 tablespoons flour**
**1 tablespoon tomato paste**
**1 cup milk**
**one 7-ounce can salmon,
   drained and flaked
   (reserve liquid), or 1 cup
   flaked cooked salmon**
**¼ cup chicken broth (if
   using cooked salmon)**
**¾ teaspoon salt**
**½ teaspoon dried dill**
**½ teaspoon crumbled
   thyme**
**⅛ teaspoon pepper**
**4 eggs, separated**
**½ cup shredded sharp
   Cheddar cheese**
**Lemon Sauce (page 93)**

1. Preheat oven to 375° F. Melt butter or margarine in large skillet. Add and sauté the chopped onion and green pepper. Stir in flour and tomato paste. Cook a few seconds until bubbly.

2. Gradually add milk and reserved salmon liquid (or ¼ cup chicken broth), stirring over low heat until mixture is thickened and smooth. Stir in ½ teaspoon of the salt, the dill, thyme and pepper.

3. Beat egg yolks; off heat, slowly stir yolks into sauce until well blended. Return to low heat and add flaked salmon and cheese; mix gently but well. Remove from heat.

4. Whip egg whites with the remaining ¼ teaspoon salt until they stand in moist peaks. Fold into salmon mixture. Turn into a greased 1½-quart soufflé dish. Bake 30 minutes. Serve at once with Lemon Sauce.

## Lemon Sauce

½ cup sour cream
½ cup unflavored yogurt
2 tablespoons lemon juice
1 teaspoon grated lemon
   rind

1. In top of double boiler over simmering water, heat together the sour cream, yogurt, lemon juice and rind.

2. Serve in small heated pitcher, stirring well just before passing alongside soufflé. *Makes about 1 cup.*

## CUCUMBER AND PEAS

1 cup fresh peas (from
   about 1 pound peas in
   pods), or one 10-ounce
   package frozen peas
1 large cucumber, pared,
   seeded and diced
1 cup shredded lettuce
¼ cup chopped parsley
½ cup water
1 teaspoon sugar
¼ teaspoon salt
¼ cup sour cream
1 tablespoon lemon juice

1. Layer peas, cucumber, lettuce and parsley in a large saucepan. Add water, sugar and salt; do not stir.

2. Cover and cook over medium heat for 10 minutes. Fold in sour cream and lemon juice; serve at once.

*TimeSaving Tip: For a menu full of vegetables, here is a host of quick tips to speed their preparation:*
• *Tear (do not cut) fresh spinach into bite-size pieces, first washing in at least two bowls of water to remove sand.*
• *Ripe pea pods will pop when both seams are pressed between finger and thumb; run thumb from stem to tip to remove peas.*
• *Shred lettuce finely with a French knife; the best varieties for shredding are crisp and firm such as iceberg, romaine and escarole.*
• *Cut corn kernels off cob by standing ear of corn in center of angel food cake pan and cutting from top to bottom with sharp knife. Work entirely around the cob and the kernels will fall into the pan.*

# BLUEFISH MENU

**COLD YOGURT SOUP**
WITH PITA TRIANGLES

**IN-AND-OUT BLUEFISH**

**AU GRATIN POTATOES**

SPINACH SALAD

LIME SHERBET
WITH BLUEBERRIES

Serves 6.

*WORK PLAN: First, prepare* **Cold Yogurt Soup.** *Toast buttered triangles of pita bread to serve with soup. Then, scoop 1 mound of lime sherbet from a quart container into each of 6 dessert dishes; freeze. At dessert time, press fresh or frozen (thawed) blueberries in circle on top; garnish edge of each circle with mint leaf. In large salad bowl, combine 6 cups bite-size pieces of spinach, 1 cup very thin onion rings and ½ cup crisply fried, crumbled bacon. (Just before dinner, toss with dressing made from ½ cup wine vinegar, ¼ cup bacon fat and ½ teaspoon pepper, heated in a skillet.) Prepare* **In-and-Out Bluefish.** *Prepare* **Au Gratin Potatoes,** *baking alongside bluefish.*

# COLD YOGURT SOUP

2 large cucumbers
salt and white pepper
1 tablespoon finely chopped
 parsley
1 tablespoon finely chopped
 chives
1 tablespoon chopped fresh
 dill, or 1½ teaspoons
 dried dill
1 large clove garlic, crushed
2 cups unflavored yogurt
½ cup chopped walnuts

1. Pare and seed cucumbers. Chop into ¼-inch dice. Place in medium bowl and sprinkle with salt and white pepper.

2. Add parsley, chives, dill and garlic.

3. Fold in yogurt and chopped walnuts. Cover with plastic wrap and chill at least 1 hour to blend flavors.

*TimeSaving Tip: Can't locate pita bread? Take thin slices of white bread, trim off crusts and brush both sides with melted butter or margarine. Toast in oven until crisp and golden, then cut into triangles.*

## IN-AND-OUT BLUEFISH

1½ cups packaged herb
   stuffing mix (from an
   8-ounce package)
1 cup butter or margarine,
   melted
1 tablespoon chopped
   parsley
1 tablespoon chopped onion
2 bluefish fillets
   (1 to 1½ pounds each)
½ pound sliced bacon
parsley
lemon wedges

1. Preheat oven to 350° F. In small bowl, combine stuffing mix, ¾ cup of the melted butter or margarine, the parsley and onion.

2. Place one of the fillets skin side down in a greased shallow baking pan. Neatly pile stuffing mixture on one fillet, distributing it evenly and leaving a small border on all sides. Place second fillet over stuffing, skin side up.

3. Starting at large end, cover both sides and top of fish bundle with bacon strips; cut bacon smaller for covering smaller end of fish. (The fish should appear striped, not completely covered with bacon.) Pour the remaining ¼ cup melted butter or margarine over top.

4. Bake 30 minutes, or until fish flakes easily with a fork and is white. Remove to a heated oblong platter and surround with bunches of parsley and lemon wedges.

## AU GRATIN POTATOES

three 11½-ounce packages
   frozen au gratin potatoes,
   thawed
1 tablespoon instant minced
   onion
1 small clove garlic, crushed
¼ teaspoon crumbled
   thyme
3 tablespoons grated sharp
   Cheddar cheese

1. In large bowl, combine thawed potatoes, minced onion, garlic and thyme. Place in greased shallow baking dish. Sprinkle cheese on top.

2. Bake in 350° F oven for 30 minutes.

# SHRIMP CHEESE MENU

SHRIMP CHEESE BAKE

NEW POTATOES
AND SWEET GHERKINS

CRUSTY BREAD

LEMON SHERBET
WITH CASSIS

SHORTBREAD COOKIES

Serves 6.

*WORK PLAN: Prepare **Shrimp Cheese Bake**. Meanwhile, divide 1 quart lemon sherbet among 6 dessert glasses; freeze. At dessert time, pour 1 tablespoon cassis (blackberry brandy) over each; serve with shortbread cookies. Prepare potatoes: Peel 1-inch band from each of 2 pounds new red or tiny white potatoes. Cook in boiling salted water until tender; drain. Serve accompanied by sweet gherkins and crusty bread with salted butter.*

## SHRIMP CHEESE BAKE

one 4-pound Edam cheese,
   peeled
1 cup finely chopped onion
2 tablespoons butter or
   margarine
1 tablespoon vegetable oil
⅓ cup well-drained canned
   tomatoes
¼ teaspoon cayenne pepper
pinch of freshly ground
   black pepper
1 pound raw shrimp, shelled
   and deveined
⅓ cup fresh bread crumbs
1 egg, well beaten
2 tablespoons golden
   raisins
1 tablespoon finely chopped
   gherkin
4 small stuffed olives, sliced

1. Cut a 1-inch slice off top of cheese to make a lid. Scoop out cheese from base and lid, leaving a ½-inch shell all around. Place cheese base and lid in cold water to cover for 30 minutes. Grate enough of the scooped-out cheese to make 2 cups. (Save remainder for another use.)

2. In small skillet over moderate heat, sauté onion in butter or margarine and oil until soft. Add tomatoes, cayenne pepper and freshly ground black pepper and cook until all juices evaporate. Add tomato mixture to the 2 cups of grated cheese, along with shrimp, bread crumbs, beaten egg, raisins, chopped gherkin and sliced olives. Mix until well blended.

3. Drain cheese base and lid; pat dry with paper towels. Place cheese base in greased 1½-quart soufflé or baking dish (at least 3 inches high). Fill base with shrimp-cheese mixture and cover with cheese lid.

4. Bake at 350° F for 35 minutes, or until brown and bubbly. Serve immediately.

# SCAMPI MENU

ARTICHOKES
WITH HOLLANDAISE
**SCAMPI**
GREEN SALAD
FRENCH BREAD
**MINTED GRAPEFRUIT**
ROLLED COOKIES

Serves 4.

*WORK PLAN: Prepare **Minted Grapefruit;** serve with rolled cookies for dessert. To prepare artichokes, cut stems from 4 artichokes; using scissors, cut off tips of leaves. Place artichokes in pressure cooker with 1 cup water, 1 tablespoon olive oil and 1 clove garlic, slivered. Tightly secure lid on pressure cooker; increase pressure according to manufacturer's directions. Cook artichokes at 15 pounds pressure for 10 minutes; cool as directed before removing the lid. (Or simmer artichokes for 45 minutes in 2 quarts water with olive oil and garlic; cool slightly.) To make hollandaise sauce, heat 1 cup mayonnaise or salad dressing, 1 egg yolk, 2 tablespoons lemon juice and 1 teaspoon grated lemon rind in top of double boiler over simmering water; stir occasionally. Keep warm. Meanwhile, combine 2 cups each bite-size pieces romaine lettuce and 1-inch sprigs of chicory in large salad bowl; chill. (Just before serving, toss with mixture of 1/3 cup olive oil, 2 tablespoons wine vinegar and 1 teaspoon each salt, sugar and dry mustard.) Prepare **Scampi,** and serve with warm French bread.*

## MINTED GRAPEFRUIT

2 large grapefruit, halved
4 teaspoons brown sugar
4 teaspoons crème de menthe

1. Loosen grapefruit segments and remove seeds.

2. Sprinkle 1 teaspoon brown sugar and 1 teaspoon crème de menthe over each grapefruit half; chill.

## SCAMPI

1½ pounds large shrimp, shelled and deveined
1 cup white wine
½ cup olive oil
1 tablespoon lemon juice
1 teaspoon salt
¼ teaspoon pepper
2 garlic cloves, crushed
2 tablespoons chopped parsley

1. Combine shrimp, wine, oil and lemon juice in a large skillet over medium heat. Stir until liquid in skillet simmers.

2. Stir in salt, pepper and garlic. Cover and simmer for 5 minutes, or until shrimp are just tender.

3. Turn into serving dish and sprinkle with parsley.

# SHRIMP-CHICKEN MENU

JELLIED MADRILENE

**SHRIMP-CHICKEN MOUNTAIN**

WHEAT PILAF

GREEN BEAN SALAD

PEACH ICE CREAM, PEACHES AND BERRY SAUCE

---

Serves 4.

**WORK PLAN:** *Divide two 10-ounce cans consommé madrilene among 4 soup cups; chill in freezer to set (take care not to freeze). Top each with 1 tablespoon sour cream and a sprinkling of chopped chives before serving. Cook 1½ pounds small whole green beans in 1 inch of boiling salted water until tender, about 5 to 8 minutes. Cool under cold running water; drain, and toss with ½ cup herb salad dressing and ¼ cup chopped fresh dill. Place on lettuce-lined platter; chill. Prepare **Shrimp-Chicken Mountain.** Heat two 16-ounce cans wheat pilaf (bulgur wheat) according to label directions. For dessert, divide 1½ pints peach ice cream among 4 dessert dishes; surround with slices from 2 ripe fresh peaches or one 8-ounce can peach slices, drained. Serve with sauce made by pureeing one 12-ounce package frozen raspberries or strawberries, slightly thawed, and ¼ cup rum.*

## SHRIMP-CHICKEN MOUNTAIN

**8 chicken breast halves, boned**
**½ cup flour**
**1 teaspoon salt**
**¼ teaspoon pepper**
**3 tablespoons olive or vegetable oil**
**1 cup chopped onion**
**⅔ cup cubed cooked ham**
**2 cloves garlic, crushed**
**2 tablespoons chopped parsley**
**¼ teaspoon paprika**
**pinch of cayenne pepper**
**1 cup dry white wine**
**16 very large, raw shrimp, shelled and deveined**
**hot wheat pilaf**
**parsley sprigs**

1. Dredge chicken pieces in mixture of flour, salt and pepper. Heat oil in large skillet; add chicken and brown on all sides. Remove from skillet and keep warm.

2. Add onion, ham and garlic to skillet. Cook until onion is soft. Add parsley, paprika and cayenne pepper. Sauté 1 minute. Pour in wine. Deglaze skillet, stirring up browned bits from bottom.

3. Return chicken to skillet; cover and reduce heat. Simmer 20 minutes, or until almost tender.

4. Place shrimp on top of chicken. Cover and simmer for 5 minutes, or until shrimp are pink and just tender. Do not overcook.

5. Arrange chicken breasts in center of large heated serving platter. Pour ham and sauce over chicken. Crown with shrimp. Surround all with wheat pilaf and sprigs of parsley. *(Shown on front cover.)*

# FIVE COOK-AHEAD DAYS

CHAPTER FOUR

**I**f you can't face cooking dinner after a full day, here's a satisfying solution: Go on a cooking spree for one day. Then when you simply have no time or energy to cook, reach into the freezer for a hearty meal that takes only minutes to heat.

This chapter includes five cook-ahead days complete with preparation charts and recipes. For each cook-ahead day you can make about ten dishes during six hours in the kitchen. The detailed charts are your guide, taking you through every stage of preparation.

For an easy and successful cook-ahead day, keep these points in mind:

- Pick a day when there will be no interruptions so you can make the best use of time, food and energy (yours and the oven's).
- Make a comprehensive shopping list. With the large quantity of food you'll be using, it pays to shop for supermarket specials.
- Plan to have leftovers to use in your cook-ahead recipes. For example, if a recipe calls for cooked rice try to serve it the night before.
- Follow the charts precisely so that the timing dovetails to your advantage. Dishes simmer on top of the stove while food is being prepared for the oven, and several dishes go into the oven at once.
- Allow extra time to cool and wrap the prepared food for freezing. Label and date all dishes so that they are used before the end of the recommended storage period.
- Adhere to the instructions for thawing and reheating food for optimum taste and safety. And never refreeze food; it should be used within two days.

Can't cook tonight? If you've "cooked ahead," a fussless, home-cooked meal can be on the table in minutes.

# COOK-AHEAD DAY ONE

| | | TO COOK | TO STORE AND SERVE |
|---|---|---|---|
| I | **Turkey Soup**<br>**Lentil Soup** | Each soup takes 15 minutes to prepare. The Turkey Soup simmers up to 8 hours; the Lentil Soup simmers up to 2 hours and requires 15 minutes additional time to complete at the end. | Cool to room temperature. Pour into plastic freezer containers, leaving ½- to ¾-inch headroom. (Liquid will expand on freezing.) Cover tightly with plastic lids. Label and freeze up to 3 months.<br><br>Thaw slightly at room temperature (or overnight in refrigerator). Heat covered over low heat to thaw completely; heat over medium heat until piping hot. (Lentil Soup must not boil.) |
| II | **Squash Casserole**<br>**Rice Medley** | Preheat oven to 325° F. The Squash Casserole takes 10 minutes to prepare, and the Rice Medley takes 5 minutes. Place squash on top shelf of oven for 45 minutes, the rice on bottom shelf for about 30 to 35 minutes. | Cool to room temperature; tightly cover tops of casseroles with heavy-duty foil. Label and freeze casseroles up to 6 months.<br><br>Thaw overnight in refrigerator; heat covered at 325° F for 15 to 20 minutes. |
| III | **Beef Pot Pie**<br>**Sweet-and-Sour**<br>   **Shrimp Casserole**<br>**Stuffed Minute**<br>   **Steaks** | Make the filling for Beef Pot Pie; this takes 40 minutes to prepare and cook, and 10 minutes to cool. Also, prepare pastry and line pie plate for pie. Prepare Sweet-and-Sour Shrimp Casserole and Stuffed Minute Steaks for baking. Each dish takes about 30 minutes to prepare. Increase oven temperature to 400° F. Bake pie on top shelf for 25 minutes. Bake shrimp and steaks side by side on bottom shelf for about 15 to 20 minutes. | Cool to room temperature. Overwrap pie in heavy-duty foil; tightly cover tops of other two dishes with foil. Label and freeze up to 6 months for pie and steaks, up to 3 months for shrimp.<br><br>Thaw in refrigerator overnight. Heat unwrapped pie at 400° F for 12 minutes or until piping hot. Heat shrimp and steaks covered at 400° F for about 12 minutes or until hot. |

| | TO COOK | TO STORE AND SERVE |
|---|---|---|
| IV **Fudge Tarts**<br>**Black and White**<br>**Cupcakes**<br>**Banana Coffee Cake** | Prepare pastry for Fudge Tarts and chill for 1 hour. Reduce oven temperature to 350° F. Make Black and White Cupcakes; preparation time is 20 minutes and baking time is 25 minutes. Prepare Banana Coffee Cake (15 minutes); bake on lower shelf of oven for 35 minutes. Finish tarts (about 20 minutes) and bake on top shelf for 25 minutes. | Cool to room temperature. Place tarts and cupcakes in freezer containers; overwrap pan containing coffee cake with heavy-duty foil. Label and freeze up to 3 months.<br><br>Thaw covered at room temperature. |

# TURKEY SOUP

leftover bones from 1 turkey
1 medium onion, quartered
1 carrot, peeled and
  quartered
1 large stalk celery,
  quartered
2 teaspoons garlic salt
2 teaspoons onion salt
2 teaspoons celery salt
one ¾-ounce envelope
  onion soup mix
⅓ cup uncooked barley
¼ cup chopped parsley
1 teaspoon crumbled basil

1. Place turkey bones in 5-quart saucepan. Add water to within 1 inch of top. Add onion, carrot, celery, garlic salt, onion salt and celery salt.

2. Bring to boiling point; cover saucepan and lower heat. Simmer, adding water as needed, for 7 hours, or until broth is rich and well flavored (no less than 2 hours).

3. Strain broth and return to saucepan. Pick meat from bones and add to broth. Add onion soup mix, barley, parsley and basil. Cook over low heat 45 minutes, or until barley is tender. *Serves 8.*

## LENTIL SOUP

one 16-ounce bag lentils
8 cups water
1 medium onion, quartered
1 medium apple, peeled,
  cored and quartered
1 carrot, peeled and cut into
  chunks
1 large stalk celery
1½ tablespoons salt
1 teaspoon crumbled
  tarragon
1 cup unflavored yogurt
2 to 3 cups chicken broth
salt and pepper to taste

1. Wash and pick over lentils. Place in 5-quart Dutch oven. Add water, onion, apple, carrot, celery, salt and tarragon.

2. Bring to boiling point; cover saucepan and reduce heat. Simmer 1½ hours, or until lentils and vegetables are tender. Cool slightly.

3. In food processor or electric blender, puree mixture, 1 cup at a time, until smooth. As mixture is pureed, pour into large glass or ceramic bowl. Stir in yogurt. Add enough chicken broth to reach desired consistency. Taste and add salt and pepper, if necessary. Reheat until very hot, but do *not* boil. *Serves 8.*

## SQUASH CASSEROLE

1 pound yellow summer
  squash, sliced and
  cooked
¼ cup chopped celery
¼ cup chopped onion
2 tablespoons butter or
  margarine
1 cup grated sharp Cheddar
  cheese
3 eggs
¾ cup milk
½ teaspoon salt
¼ teaspoon ground allspice
⅛ teaspoon cayenne pepper

1. Preheat oven to 325° F. Place cooked squash in greased 2-quart casserole.

2. In small skillet over moderately high heat, sauté celery and onion in butter or margarine until tender. Pour over squash. Sprinkle with cheese.

3. In small bowl, beat together eggs, milk, salt, allspice and cayenne pepper. Pour over cheese. Bake 45 minutes, or until top is golden and bubbly hot. *Serves 4.*

## RICE MEDLEY

2¼ cups water
2 cups quick-cooking rice
half of ¾-ounce envelope
  onion soup mix
one 10-ounce package
  frozen Hawaiian-style
  vegetables with pineapple
  in sauce, slightly thawed

1. Preheat oven to 325° F. In greased 1½-quart casserole, combine water, rice and onion soup mix. Cover with aluminum foil.

2. Bake 20 minutes. Stir in vegetables. Bake 10 to 15 minutes longer, or until liquid is absorbed and vegetables and rice are tender. *Serves 4 to 6.*

## BEEF POT PIE

1 pound lean beef, cut into
   1-inch cubes
⅓ cup flour
¾ teaspoon salt
¼ teaspoon pepper
2 tablespoons bacon
   drippings or vegetable oil
1½ cups water
1 teaspoon crumbled basil
1 teaspoon dried parsley
1 teaspoon instant minced
   onion
1 cup diced carrots
1 cup diced peeled potatoes
one 10-ounce package
   frozen peas
two 9- to 11-ounce
   packages piecrust mix
1 egg
1 tablespoon milk

1. Dredge beef with mixture of flour, salt and pepper. Brown beef in bacon drippings or vegetable oil in medium saucepan over moderately high heat. Add water, basil, parsley and minced onion. Bring to boiling point; cover saucepan and lower heat. Simmer 20 minutes, or until meat is almost tender.

2. Uncover saucepan. Add carrots, potato and frozen peas. Continue cooking just until vegetables are tender when pierced with a fork. Cool mixture.

3. Preheat oven to 400° F. Prepare piecrust mix according to label directions. Roll out two-thirds of the pastry to a 13-inch circle on a lightly floured board; fit into 10-inch pie plate. Trim overhang to ½ inch. Spoon beef mixture into dish. Roll out remaining pastry to a 12-inch circle. Cover beef filling with top pastry and cut several long slits in top to let steam escape. Trim overhang to 1 inch; turn under flush with rim and flute.

4. In a cup, beat egg slightly with milk. Brush over top pastry. Bake 25 minutes, or until pastry is golden brown and filling is bubbly hot. *Serves 6.*

## SWEET-AND-SOUR SHRIMP CASSEROLE

2 cups quick-cooking rice
1½ pounds shrimp, shelled
   and deveined
1¾ cups dry white wine
1 tablespoon soy sauce
1 teaspoon salt
¾ cup brown sugar, firmly
   packed
¾ cup chopped celery
¾ cup chopped carrot
one 8-ounce can pineapple
   chunks and syrup
¼ cup ketchup
green pepper rings

1. Place rice in bottom of 2-quart casserole. In large bowl, marinate shrimp in 1 cup of the wine, the soy sauce and salt for 15 minutes, turning once or twice. Pour over rice in casserole.

2. Preheat oven to 400° F. In medium saucepan, combine the remaining ¾ cup wine, the brown sugar, celery, carrot, pineapple with syrup, and ketchup. Bring to boiling point; lower heat and simmer 10 minutes, or until vegetables are barely tender. Pour over shrimp and rice.

3. Cover and bake 20 minutes, or until shrimp, rice and vegetables are tender. Garnish with green pepper rings. *Serves 4 to 6.*

# STUFFED MINUTE STEAKS

one 6¾-ounce package
   long-grain and wild rice
   mix
½ cup chopped celery
½ cup chopped onion
⅓ cup butter or margarine
10 large minute steaks
salt and pepper to taste

1. Cook long-grain and wild rice mix according to label directions.

2. In medium skillet over moderately high heat, sauté celery and onion in 3 tablespoons of the butter or margarine for 5 minutes, or until soft. Stir in cooked rice with a fork until well blended.

3. Preheat oven to 400° F. Sprinkle steaks with salt and pepper. Spoon rice stuffing on each steak, dividing evenly. Roll up jelly-roll fashion, then tie well with string. Place seam side down in greased 13 x 9 x 2-inch baking pan. Dot with remaining butter or margarine.

4. Bake for 15 minutes, or until meat is brown and stuffing is hot. *Serves 4 or 5.*

# FUDGE TARTS

**CREAM CHEESE PASTRY**
one 8-ounce package cream
   cheese, softened
1⅓ cups butter or
   margarine, softened
3 cups flour

**FUDGE FILLING**
one 6-ounce package
   semisweet chocolate
   morsels
¼ cup crème de cacao
½ cup sweetened
   condensed milk
¼ teaspoon salt

1. Make cream cheese pastry: In medium bowl, combine cream cheese, butter or margarine and flour until well blended. Form into a ball. Wrap in waxed paper. Chill for about 1 hour.

2. Make fudge filling: In top of double boiler, melt chocolate morsels in crème de cacao. Stir in sweetened condensed milk and salt.

3. Preheat oven to 350° F. Roll out chilled dough ⅛ inch thick on lightly floured board. Cut into 2-inch circles and fit into 18 to 20 one-inch tart pans.

4. Spoon filling into pastry-lined pans, dividing evenly and filling no more than two-thirds full. Bake 25 minutes, or until pastry is golden and filling is set.

5. Cool in pans on wire racks for 3 minutes. Gently loosen from pans, using a metal skewer or point of narrow-bladed knife; remove from pans and cool completely on wire racks. *Makes 18 to 20 tarts.*

## BLACK AND WHITE CUPCAKES

one 8-ounce package cream
  cheese, softened
1 egg
⅓ cup sugar
⅛ teaspoon salt
one 6-ounce package
  semisweet chocolate
  morsels
1½ cups flour
1 cup sugar
⅓ cup unsweetened cocoa
  powder
1 teaspoon baking soda
½ teaspoon salt
1 cup warm water
⅓ cup butter or margarine,
  melted
1 tablespoon vinegar
1 teaspoon vanilla extract
½ cup chopped pecans
½ cup sugar
½ teaspoon cinnamon

1. Preheat oven to 350° F. Grease 18 to 20 two-inch cupcake tins, or use paper liners.

2. In small bowl, beat together cream cheese, egg, ⅓ cup sugar and ⅛ teaspoon salt until light and fluffy. Add chocolate morsels.

3. Into large bowl, sift flour, 1 cup sugar, cocoa, baking soda and ½ teaspoon salt. In 2-cup measure, mix warm water, melted butter or margarine, vinegar and vanilla extract. Add to flour mixture and stir just until blended.

4. Pour cocoa batter into prepared tins, filling each no more than half full. Top each with 1 tablespoon cream cheese mixture. Sprinkle with mixture of chopped pecans, ½ cup sugar and the cinnamon.

5. Bake 25 minutes, or until cocoa batter springs back when gently pressed with fingertip. Cool in tins on wire rack 5 minutes. Gently loosen from tins with long sharp knife. Remove from tins and cool completely on wire rack. *Makes 18 to 20 cupcakes.*

## BANANA COFFEE CAKE

2 cups flour
1 teaspoon salt
1 teaspoon baking soda
1 teaspoon baking powder
¾ cup butter or margarine,
  softened
1½ cups sugar
3 eggs
about 1½ cups mashed
  bananas
1 teaspoon vanilla extract
⅔ cup creamed cottage
  cheese

GLAZE
1 cup confectioners' sugar
2 tablespoons butter or
  margarine
2 tablespoons frozen orange
  juice concentrate

1. Preheat oven to 350° F. Sift flour, salt, baking soda and baking powder onto waxed paper.

2. Place ¾ cup softened butter or margarine and 1½ cups sugar in medium bowl; beat with electric mixer at high speed until light and fluffy. Beat in eggs, one at a time, beating well after each addition.

3. In small bowl, combine mashed bananas with vanilla extract and cottage cheese. Add to butter mixture alternately with dry ingredients, beginning and ending with dry ingredients. Spoon into greased 13 x 9 x 2-inch baking pan.

4. Bake 35 minutes, or until wooden skewer inserted in center comes out clean. Cool in pan on wire rack for about 15 minutes.

5. Meanwhile, make glaze: In a small saucepan, combine 1 cup confectioners' sugar, 2 tablespoons butter or margarine and orange juice concentrate. Bring to boiling point over moderately low heat, stirring often. Pour over warm cake. *Serves 12.*

# COOK-AHEAD DAY TWO

| | | TO COOK | TO STORE AND SERVE |
|---|---|---|---|
| I | **Navy Bean Soup**<br>**Double Vegetable**<br>**Bisque**<br>**Pennsylvania Creamy**<br>**Potato Soup** | The night before, soak beans for Navy Bean Soup; finish preparation the next day (about 5 minutes). The bean soup takes up to 2 hours to cook and requires 15 additional minutes at the end. The Double Vegetable Bisque cooks in 15 minutes and requires 15 additional minutes. While vegetables for bisque are cooking, cook bacon, potatoes and onion for Pennsylvania Creamy Potato Soup (about 25 minutes). Puree bisque vegetables as directed, then complete Pennsylvania Creamy Potato Soup (about 15 minutes more). | Cool to room temperature. Pour into plastic freezer containers, leaving ½- to ¾-inch headroom. (Liquid will expand on freezing.) Cover tightly with plastic lids. Label and freeze up to 3 months.<br>Thaw slightly at room temperature (or overnight in refrigerator). Heat covered over low heat to thaw completely; heat over medium heat until piping hot. Complete bisque as directed in recipe. (Bisque and potato soup must not boil.) |
| II | **Sweet Potato**<br>**Puffle**<br>**Carrot Soufflé** | Cook sweet potatoes and carrots for Sweet Potato Puffle and Carrot Soufflé (40 minutes). Preheat oven to 350° F. Finish preparing both dishes (15 minutes for each); place soufflé on bottom shelf of oven for about 45 minutes and puffle on top shelf for about 30 minutes. | Cool to room temperature. Tightly cover tops of dishes with heavy-duty foil. Label and freeze up to 3 months.<br>Thaw overnight in refrigerator. Heat dishes covered at 350° F for 15 to 20 minutes (set soufflé in a roasting pan of boiling water). |

| | | TO COOK | TO STORE AND SERVE |
|---|---|---|---|
| III | **Baked Chili** **Baked Ham Loaf** **Shell Macaroni Casserole** | Prepare three main dishes (each takes 15 to 20 minutes). Place Baked Chili on bottom shelf of 350° F oven for about 1½ hours. Place Baked Ham Loaf on top shelf for about 1 hour. Bake Shell Macaroni Casserole on top shelf beside ham for about 35 minutes. Remove chili from oven after 1½ hours and increase temperature to 450° F. Add the browned flour and caraway seeds; arrange biscuit topping over the chili. Bake on top shelf for 10 to 12 minutes. | Cool to room temperature. Tightly cover tops with heavy-duty foil. Label and freeze chili and macaroni up to 6 months, ham loaf up to 3 months. Thaw in refrigerator overnight. Heat chili covered at 350° F for 25 minutes or until piping hot. Heat the ham loaf and the macaroni covered at 350° F for 15 minutes or until hot. |
| IV | **Marzipan Tarts** **Creamy Chocolate Cheese Pie** | Prepare pastry for Marzipan Tarts and chill for 1 hour. Lower oven temperature to 375° F. Make crumb crust for Creamy Chocolate Cheese Pie. Bake on top shelf of oven for 10 minutes; cool. Finish preparing tarts (20 minutes) and bake for 25 minutes. Prepare filling for pie (10 minutes), fill crumb crust and freeze for 4 hours before serving or wrapping for storage. | Cool tarts to room temperature. Place in freezer containers. Label and freeze up to 3 months. Freeze pie until firm, then overwrap with heavy-duty foil; label and freeze up to 3 months. Thaw tarts covered at room temperature. Thaw pie 10 minutes at room temperature for easier slicing. |

## NAVY BEAN SOUP

one 16-ounce bag navy
  beans
10 cups water
1 ham bone
3 stalks celery, quartered
1 large onion, quartered
1 large carrot, peeled and
  quartered
3 tablespoons ketchup
1 tablespoon salt
1 teaspoon pepper
1 clove garlic, slivered
1 tablespoon chopped fresh
  parsley

1. Place beans in colander and rinse well under cool running water. Pick over, removing withered beans and stones. Place beans in 5-quart kettle with water to cover. Let stand overnight.

2. Drain beans and return to kettle. Add the 10 cups water, ham bone, celery, onion, carrot, ketchup, salt, pepper, garlic and parsley. Bring to boiling point. Lower heat and cover kettle.

3. Simmer 2 hours, or until vegetables and beans are tender. Remove large pieces of vegetables and ham bone from soup; set aside. Cool soup until lukewarm. In electric blender, puree soup, 1 cup at a time. Return to kettle. Chop meat from ham bone and cut large pieces of vegetables into bite-size pieces. Return to soup. Heat slowly. *Serves 8.*

## DOUBLE VEGETABLE BISQUE

1 pound broccoli,
  broken in sprigs
1 small head cauliflower,
  broken in sprigs
2 cups chicken broth
1 cup heavy cream
1 teaspoon crumbled
  tarragon
flavored croutons

1. Cook broccoli and cauliflower separately in boiling salted water to cover until tender, about 10 to 15 minutes. Drain.

2. In electric blender, puree broccoli and cauliflower, a little at a time. As each batch is pureed, place in 1½-quart freezer container. Stir in chicken broth. Label and freeze.

3. At serving time: Place slightly thawed mixture in a medium saucepan; heat covered over low heat to thaw completely. Stir in cream and tarragon. Heat gently, but do *not* boil. Serve bisque in bowls with croutons sprinkled on top. *Serves 4 to 6.*

*Note:* You can use 2 cups each leftover cooked broccoli and cauliflower sprigs.

# PENNSYLVANIA CREAMY POTATO SOUP

3 slices bacon
2 large potatoes, peeled and
  quartered
1 small onion, quartered
4 cups milk
⅔ cup flour
½ teaspoon salt
1 egg
salt and freshly ground
  pepper to taste

1. Sauté bacon until crisp in small skillet over moderately high heat. Drain on paper towels; crumble. Reserve 2 tablespoons of the bacon drippings.

2. In medium saucepan, cook potatoes and onion in boiling salted water until tender when pierced with a fork. Drain in colander. Return to saucepan and mash slightly. Pour in milk and the reserved 2 tablespoons of bacon drippings. Cook over moderately low heat just until milk starts to boil. Lower heat.

3. In small bowl, mix flour and salt; make a well in the center. Break egg into well. Stir with a fork until small balls form. Add dumpling dough to hot milk and potatoes, stirring to mix well. Keep soup just below boiling point for 10 minutes, or until soup is thickened and dumplings are cooked. Sprinkle crumbled bacon on top. Season with salt and pepper. *Serves 4.*

*Note:* The dumplings can be frozen along with the soup, but for absolutely perfect results, try this: Remove dumplings from the soup with a slotted spoon; drain and freeze separately in a small plastic freezer container.

*TimeSaving Tip: Dried beans or peas that will be used in a soup should first be soaked overnight in water. To cut down on this preparation time, place the dried beans or peas in a large saucepan; cover with 2½ times their volume of water and boil for 2 minutes. Remove from heat; cover tightly and let stand for 1 hour. All the water should be absorbed; then, proceed as directed in recipe.*
• *To speed up cooking time of soups, cut up all ingredients finely and cook only until the ingredients are tender; the results will be tasty, although the flavor may not be as fully developed.*
• *To save money, make croutons for soup from day-old bread. Trim off crusts and dice bread into ¼-inch cubes; sauté in 2 tablespoons butter or margarine or vegetable oil for every cup of bread cubes. Or toast in hot oven until golden.*
• *To save time and energy when cooking frozen food, heat food in a microwave oven according to manufacturer's directions; make sure the food is in a nonmetal dish and is covered with plastic wrap or waxed paper.*

## SWEET POTATO PUFFLE

3 medium-size sweet
  potatoes or yams
2 cups boiling water
1 teaspoon salt
½ cup brown sugar, firmly
  packed
3 eggs, separated
¼ cup orange liqueur or
  orange juice
3 tablespoons butter or
  margarine
pinch of salt

1. Scrub potatoes well under cold water. Cut off root end and any bruised spots. Place in large saucepan. Add 2 cups boiling water and 1 teaspoon salt.

2. Bring to boiling point; cover. Cook 35 to 40 minutes, or until just tender when pierced with a fork. Drain and let stand until cool enough to handle; peel.

3. Preheat oven to 350° F. Place potatoes in a medium bowl. Mash or beat with an electric mixer until smooth. Stir in brown sugar, egg yolks, orange liqueur or orange juice, butter or margarine, and a pinch of salt until well blended.

4. Using electric mixer at high speed, beat egg whites in small bowl until stiff. Fold into potato mixture. Spoon into greased 1½-quart soufflé dish.

5. Bake 30 minutes, or until puffy and browned on top. Serve immediately. *Serves 4 to 6.*

## CARROT SOUFFLE

4 cups sliced cooked
  carrots
2 eggs, separated
2 tablespoons butter or
  margarine, softened
2 tablespoons brown sugar,
  firmly packed
1 teaspoon salt
½ teaspoon mace or
  nutmeg
¾ teaspoon cornstarch
⅓ cup cold milk

1. Preheat oven to 350° F. In electric blender, puree carrots, a little at a time, at high speed until smooth. Pour into large bowl. Stir in egg yolks, butter or margarine, brown sugar, salt, and mace or nutmeg until well blended.

2. In a 1-cup measure, stir cornstarch into milk until dissolved. Stir into carrot puree. Heat for about 1 minute, stirring constantly.

3. Using electric mixer at high speed, beat egg whites in small bowl until stiff. Fold into carrot puree. Spoon mixture into greased 1½-quart soufflé dish or casserole. Place dish in roasting pan on oven rack. Pour boiling water into roasting pan to a depth of 2 inches.

4. Bake 45 minutes, or until puffy and golden. Serve immediately. *Serves 4 to 6.*

# BAKED CHILI

1 pound ground chuck
2 cups sliced onion
1 tablespoon chili powder
one 28-ounce can whole
 tomatoes
one 16-ounce can red
 kidney beans
1 teaspoon salt
2 tablespoons flour
1 teaspoon caraway seeds

**BISCUIT TOPPING**
1½ cups buttermilk biscuit
 mix
½ cup white stoneground
 cornmeal
½ cup milk

1. Shape ground chuck into a large patty. Brown for 5 minutes per side in large skillet. Crumble into small pieces; remove with slotted spoon to paper towels. When drained, place in a 2-quart casserole.

2. Pour off all but ¼ cup drippings from skillet. Sauté onion in drippings until almost soft. Stir in chili powder. Continue cooking 1 minute longer, or until onion is tender. Add to ground chuck in casserole.

3. Stir in tomatoes, beans and their liquid, and salt. Cover casserole loosely with aluminum foil. Bake at 350° F for about 1½ hours; remove from oven. Increase oven temperature to 450° F.

4. In small skillet over moderate heat, brown flour with caraway seeds. Stir into casserole.

5. Make biscuit topping: In small bowl, combine biscuit mix, cornmeal and milk until mixture forms a soft dough that leaves sides of bowl. Turn out onto lightly floured board. Roll out ½ inch thick; cut into 3-inch circles. Place circles of biscuit dough on top of chili.

6. Bake chili 10 to 12 minutes longer, or until biscuits are golden. *Serves 6.*

*TimeSaving Tip: While the prolonged baking of the chili in the recipe above develops the flavor, when you're in a hurry the topping can be added after only 30 minutes in the oven, and the dish will be ready to serve in less than 45 minutes total cooking time. There is always debate on the type of meat to use in chili; tiny ¼-inch cubes of beef chuck and even cubes of leftover roast beef are alternates to ground chuck. The quantity of chili powder (and whether mild or hot) depends on personal taste. Remember, chili powder should always be sautéed in oil or pan drippings to cook out its raw taste.*

*Here's how to precook vegetables for a large vegetable dish (such as the sweet potatoes and carrots on page 110) in the fastest way possible: Simply peel and cut the vegetable into thin slices; boil in ½ inch of unsalted water until tender. This usually take no longer than 10 minutes. Drain and mash while hot. Add no additional seasoning at this time; all seasonings are added to the main dish. If you're using leftover vegetables, adjust the salt level in the main dish.*

## BAKED HAM LOAF

1 pound ground smoked
   ham, uncooked
½ pound bulk sausage meat
2 cups dry seasoned bread
   crumbs
1 cup milk
2 eggs, beaten
1 teaspoon crumbled basil
1 teaspoon instant minced
   onion
1 teaspoon dried parsley
½ teaspoon salt
½ teaspoon pepper
½ cup crushed pineapple,
   drained (from an 8-ounce
   can)
¼ cup brown sugar, firmly
   packed
1 tablespoon vinegar
1 teaspoon Dijon-style
   mustard

1. In large bowl, mix ham, sausage, bread crumbs, milk, beaten eggs, basil, minced onion, parsley, salt and pepper just until well blended. Pack into greased 9 x 5 x 3-inch loaf pan, leveling off top of mixture. Bake at 350° F for about 35 minutes; pour off excess fat.

2. In 1-cup measure, combine pineapple, brown sugar, vinegar and mustard. Spoon over top of ham loaf.

3. Bake 30 minutes longer, or until firm. Let stand 5 minutes. Invert onto heated serving platter and slice. *Serves 6.*

## SHELL MACARONI CASSEROLE

one 8-ounce package small
   shell macaroni
boiling salted water
1 pound ground beef
½ cup chopped onion
salt and pepper to taste
2 cups shredded mozzarella
   cheese
1 cup shredded Gruyère
   cheese
1 cup sour cream
1 tablespoon chopped
   parsley
3 cups spaghetti sauce

1. In large saucepan, cook macaroni in boiling salted water according to label directions; drain in colander.

2. Shape ground beef into a large patty. Brown 5 minutes per side in large skillet. Crumble into small pieces; remove with slotted spoon to paper towels to drain.

3. Pour off all but 1 tablespoon drippings. In same skillet, sauté onion in drippings until soft. Stir in salt and pepper.

4. In medium bowl, combine mozzarella and Gruyère cheese, sour cream and parsley until well blended.

5. In greased 2-quart casserole, layer half each of the spaghetti sauce, macaroni, ground beef, onion, and cheese mixture; repeat layering. Cover casserole with aluminum foil. Bake at 350° F for 30 minutes; uncover casserole. Bake 5 minutes longer, or until cheese melts and sauce is bubbly hot. *Serves 6.*

## MARZIPAN TARTS

Cream Cheese Pastry (see
  Fudge Tarts, page 104)

MARZIPAN FILLING
4 ounces almond paste
  (from an 8-ounce
  package)
2 tablespoons butter or
  margarine, softened
½ cup sweetened
  condensed milk
2 eggs
2 tablespoons lemon juice
½ teaspoon almond extract

⅓ cup slivered almonds

1. Prepare cream cheese pastry; chill for 1 hour, then roll out and fit into 18 to 20 tart pans, following directions in Fudge Tarts recipe.

2. Make marzipan filling: Using electric mixer at high speed, cream almond paste with softened butter or margarine in small bowl until smooth and creamy. Beat in sweetened condensed milk, eggs, lemon juice and almond extract.

3. Preheat oven to 375° F. Spoon filling into pastry-lined pans, dividing evenly and filling no more than two-thirds full. Sprinkle with slivered almonds.

4. Bake 25 minutes, or until pastry is golden and filling is set. Cool in pans on wire racks for 5 minutes. Gently loosen from pans, using a metal skewer or point of narrow-bladed knife; remove from pans and cool completely on wire racks. *Makes 18 to 20 tarts.*

## CREAMY CHOCOLATE CHEESE PIE

1½ cups graham cracker
  crumbs
¼ cup sugar
⅓ cup butter or margarine,
  melted
one 8-ounce package cream
  cheese, softened
3 eggs, separated
⅓ cup unsweetened cocoa
  powder
1 tablespoon butter or
  margarine
1 teaspoon vanilla extract
½ teaspoon salt
1 cup heavy cream
whipped cream (optional)
shaved chocolate (optional)

1. Preheat oven to 375° F. In small bowl, combine graham cracker crumbs, sugar and the ⅓ cup melted butter or margarine. Press firmly into a 9-inch pie plate. Bake 10 minutes. Cool in refrigerator while preparing filling.

2. Using electric mixer at high speed, combine cream cheese, egg yolks, cocoa powder, the 1 tablespoon butter or margarine, vanilla extract and salt in large bowl until light and fluffy. Thoroughly wash and dry beaters.

3. Using electric mixer at high speed, whip egg whites in medium bowl until stiff peaks form. Whip heavy cream until stiff. Fold egg whites, then whipped cream, into chocolate mixture. Pour into cooled crumb crust.

4. Freeze pie 4 hours or longer before serving. Garnish with whipped cream and shaved chocolate, if you wish. *Serves 8.*

# COOK-AHEAD DAY THREE

| | TO COOK | TO STORE AND SERVE |
|---|---|---|
| **I**   **Beef Stew Orientale**<br>**Sausage in**<br>   **Mushroom Sauce**<br>**Chicken Curry**<br>**Chinese Chicken**<br>**Ham-Stuffed**<br>   **Cabbage Rolls** | Prepare Beef Stew Orientale and simmer up to 2 hours; prepare Sausage in Mushroom Sauce and simmer for 45 minutes. (Each dish takes 15 minutes to prepare for simmering.) The three remaining dishes (Chicken Curry, Chinese Chicken and Ham-Stuffed Cabbage Rolls) are made from precooked or leftover meat. Make one at a time; each.one takes 10 to 15 minutes to prepare and cook. | Cool to room temperature. Spoon all but cabbage rolls into plastic freezer containers, leaving ½- to ¾-inch headroom. (Mixture will expand on freezing.) Cover tightly with plastic lids. Label and freeze. Place cabbage rolls in baking dish; cover with heavy-duty foil, label and freeze. Freeze beef stew up to 6 months, the rest up to 3 months.<br><br>    For all but the cabbage rolls, thaw slightly at room temperature. Heat covered over low heat to thaw completely; heat over medium heat until piping hot and serve as directed. (Chicken Curry must not boil.) Thaw the cabbage rolls overnight in refrigerator and heat in oven as directed. |
| **II**   **Two-for-One Bread**<br>**Double-Good**<br>   **Yeast Rolls** | Prepare the bread doughs for Two-for-One Bread and Double-Good Yeast Rolls. Each recipe takes about 20 minutes to prepare for rising; let doughs rise for 1 to 1½ hours, as directed. | |

|  | TO COOK | TO STORE AND SERVE |
|---|---|---|
| III **Acorn Squash Bake**<br>**Broccoli Cheese**<br>**Bake** | Prepare Acorn Squash Bake and Broccoli Cheese Bake for the oven (about 5 minutes for each). Bake squash on bottom shelf of oven at 325° F for 50 minutes and broccoli on top shelf for 45 minutes. | Cool to room temperature. Wrap acorn squash halves individually in heavy-duty foil; tightly cover top of Broccoli Cheese Bake with heavy-duty foil. Label vegetables and freeze up to 3 months.<br>    Thaw overnight in refrigerator. Heat wrapped squash halves and broccoli covered at 325° F for 20 minutes or until hot. |
| IV **Two-for-One-Bread**<br>**(page 114)**<br>**Double-Good Yeast**<br>**Rolls (page 114)**<br>**Apple Cheese Tarts** | Shape bread loaves and rolls (a total of 30 minutes); let rise for 1 hour. Increase oven temperature to 425° F and prepare Apple Cheese Tarts. These take 20 minutes to prepare and 40 minutes to bake (reduce oven temperature to 375° F after first 10 minutes). After rising, bake rolls at 375° F on top shelf for 15 minutes; bake bread loaves on bottom shelf for 30 to 40 minutes. | Cool bread and rolls to room temperature. Wrap bread loaves separately in heavy-duty foil. Wrap rolls in heavy-duty foil in two batches (or place each batch in plastic freezer bag and seal, pressing out air). Cool tarts in muffin pans; cover tightly with heavy-duty foil. Label and freeze baked goods up to 6 months.<br>    Thaw covered at room temperature. Heat wrapped loaves and rolls at 300° F for 10 to 15 minutes, if desired. Heat Apple Cheese Tarts uncovered at 375° F for 12 minutes or until warm, if desired. |

*(Cook-Ahead Day Three shown on pages 86 and 87.)*

## BEEF STEW ORIENTALE

1 pound lean beef, cut into
  1-inch cubes
⅓ cup flour
¾ teaspoon salt
¼ teaspoon pepper
¼ cup bacon fat or
  vegetable oil
½ cup Burgundy wine
3 cups water
1 clove garlic, halved
1 teaspoon dried parsley
3 large carrots, cut into
  1-inch chunks
½ pound small white
  onions, peeled
one 5-ounce can water
  chestnuts, drained and
  halved
1 cup cherry tomatoes
one 6-ounce package frozen
  Chinese snow peas
hot cooked rice or Chinese
  noodles

1. Dredge beef with mixture of flour, salt and pepper. In large heavy skillet over moderately high heat, brown meat on all sides in bacon fat or vegetable oil. Place browned beef in large saucepan.

2. Pour wine over beef; add 3 cups water, garlic and parsley. Bring to boiling point. Lower heat and cover saucepan. Simmer 1½ hours, or until meat is almost tender.

3. Uncover saucepan. Add carrots and onions; continue cooking just until meat and vegetables are tender when pierced with a fork.

4. Add water chestnuts, cherry tomatoes and frozen pea pods. Simmer 5 minutes longer, or until peas are heated through. Do not overcook vegetables. They should be crisp and colorful. Serve with rice or Chinese noodles. *Serves 4.*

## SAUSAGE IN MUSHROOM SAUCE

1½ pounds sweet Italian
  sausage, or ¾ pound
  sweet and ¾ pound hot
  Italian sausage
2 tablespoons vegetable oil
½ cup chopped green
  pepper
½ cup chopped onion
1 cup sliced mushrooms
one 29-ounce can tomato
  sauce
¼ cup chopped parsley
1 teaspoon sugar
½ teaspoon crumbled basil
salt and pepper to taste

1. Cut sausage into 2-inch pieces. Brown sausage in oil in heavy skillet over moderately high heat. Remove with a slotted spoon to a 2-quart saucepan.

2. Add green pepper and onion to drippings in skillet; sauté 2 minutes. Add mushrooms. Continue sautéeing 3 minutes longer, or until vegetables are tender but not brown. Place in saucepan.

3. Stir in tomato sauce, parsley, sugar, basil, and salt and pepper. Bring to boiling point. Lower heat and cover saucepan. Simmer 45 minutes, or until flavors have blended and sauce is slightly thickened. Spoon over pasta or into Italian rolls. *Serves 4 to 6.*

## CHICKEN CURRY

**3 tablespoons butter or
   margarine**
**3 tablespoons flour**
**1 tablespoon curry powder**
**1½ cups chicken broth**
**½ cup light cream**
**salt and pepper to taste**
**2 cups cubed cooked
   chicken**
**hot cooked rice**
**½ cup chopped peanuts**
**½ cup raisins**
**½ cup coconut**
**mango chutney**

1. Melt butter or margarine in large heavy saucepan over moderately low heat. Stir in flour and curry powder until mixture is smooth. Cook and stir 1 minute.

2. Gradually pour in chicken broth. Cook over moderate heat, stirring constantly, until mixture thickens and bubbles, about 3 minutes.

3. Stir in light cream. Taste and season with salt and pepper, if needed.

4. Add cooked chicken. Heat, but do *not* boil. Serve over rice; pass separate small bowls of peanuts, raisins, coconut and chutney. *Serves 4.*

## CHINESE CHICKEN

**4 slices bacon, chopped**
**¼ cup chopped onion**
**¼ cup chopped green
   pepper**
**½ cup sliced mushrooms**
**1 cup bean sprouts**
**2 cups cubed cooked
   chicken**
**2 cups chicken broth**
**2 tablespoons cornstarch**
**hot cooked rice**
**soy sauce (optional)**

1. In wok or large skillet over moderately high heat, sauté chopped bacon until crisp. Remove bacon with a slotted spoon and drain on paper towels.

2. Add onion and green pepper to drippings in wok. Sauté, stirring often, for 3 minutes, or until soft; push to one side. Add mushrooms and sauté 2 minutes; push to one side. Add bean sprouts and sauté 2 minutes. Stir in cooked chicken and mix with vegetables. Cook 1 minute.

3. In small bowl, combine chicken broth with cornstarch until smooth. Stir into wok. Cook, stirring often, until mixture thickens and bubbles, about 3 minutes. Sprinkle with chopped bacon. Serve over hot cooked rice, with soy sauce as a condiment if desired. *Serves 4.*

# HAM-STUFFED CABBAGE ROLLS

8 cabbage leaves
½ cup sliced mushrooms
¼ cup chopped onion
¼ cup chopped green
pepper
2 tablespoons butter or
margarine
1 cup cubed cooked ham
1 cup cooked rice
one 8-ounce can tomato
sauce
¾ teaspoon sugar

1. In large saucepan, cook cabbage in boiling salted water for 2 minutes, or until leaves are pliable. Cool in colander under cold running water until easy to handle. Cut base of large vein from each leaf and discard; spread leaves flat.

2. In small skillet over moderate heat, sauté mushrooms, onion and green pepper in butter or margarine until tender.

3. Grind ham, or chop very finely. Place in medium bowl. Add cooked rice and sautéed vegetables. Mix until well blended.

4. Divide filling evenly among cabbage leaves. Fold sides in and roll up loosely. Place in greased 12 x 8 x 2-inch baking dish. In small bowl, mix tomato sauce and sugar. Pour over cabbage rolls. Cover with heavy-duty aluminum foil. Label and freeze.

5. At serving time: Bake thawed cabbage rolls covered at 375° F for 25 minutes. Uncover and bake 10 minutes longer, or until bubbly hot. *Serves 4.*

*TimeSaving Tip: A little time spent in the correct wrapping, labeling and freezing of cook-ahead dishes will reap dividends in saving time and energy later.*
* *Pourable, spoonable soups and stews store best in plastic freezer containers. Leave about ³/₄ inch of headroom to allow for liquids to expand.*
* *Press plastic lids tightly in place, or cover and seal with heavy-duty foil and freezer tape.*
* *Roasts and baked goods should be wrapped in heavy-duty foil with a double-folded seam seal (sometimes called the "drugstore" fold). Press out all air when you seal.*
* *To bring cooking dishes back into immediate circulation, line with a double layer of heavy-duty foil, greasing the dish well before lining. Freeze food in dish, then lift frozen food and its surrounding foil liner from the dish and overwrap the food again with foil.*
* *Imperfectly sealed food is liable to wind up with "freezer burn." The surface of the food turns gray and pale in color and is usually coated with ice crystals. When thawed and reheated, the food may be dehydrated, flavorless and tough.*
* *Label all food with name of dish, date of storage and the date by which it should be used. Pork products freeze up to about 2 months, poultry up to 6 months, beef up to 12 months.*

# TWO-FOR-ONE BREAD

1 cup milk
¼ cup butter or margarine
2 tablespoons sugar
2 teaspoons salt
2 envelopes active dry yeast
1½ cups very warm water
about 6 cups flour
1 cup whole wheat flour
1 cup instant potato flakes
Butterscotch Filling (below)
½ cup dried currants or dark
  raisins
1 egg white
1 teaspoon water
1 tablespoon sesame seeds

1. In small saucepan, combine milk, butter or margarine, sugar and salt. Cook over low heat until butter melts and sugar dissolves; cool.

2. In large bowl, dissolve yeast in very warm water. (Very warm water feels comfortably warm when dropped on wrist.) Stir in cooled milk mixture. Beat in 2 cups of the flour with a wooden spoon. Beat in the whole wheat flour, potato flakes and enough additional flour to make a stiff dough.

3. Turn out onto a lightly floured board. Knead 8 to 10 minutes, or until dough is smooth and elastic. (Or, beat for 5 minutes with dough hook attachment of electric mixer.)

4. Place in greased large bowl. Turn dough once to grease all sides. Cover with damp cloth. Let rise in warm place free from drafts for 1 to 1½ hours, or until doubled in bulk. Punch dough down; divide in half. Knead each half lightly for 2 minutes.

5. Shape half of dough into a loaf. Place loaf in a greased 9 x 5 x 3-inch loaf pan.

6. Prepare Butterscotch Filling. Roll remaining dough into a 9 x 15-inch rectangle. Spread slightly cooled Butterscotch Filling over dough. Top with currants or dark raisins. Roll up jelly-roll fashion, starting from narrow end. Place in another greased 9 x 5 x 3-inch loaf pan.

7. Cover loaves with damp cloth. Let rise 1 hour, or until doubled in bulk. Towards end of rising, preheat oven to 375° F. In a 1-cup measure, beat egg white and 1 teaspoon water. Brush over loaves. Sprinkle sesame seeds over the plain loaf.

8. Bake 30 to 40 minutes, or until loaves are golden brown and sound hollow when tapped. Cool in pans on wire rack 10 minutes. Loosen with long narrow knife; invert onto wire rack and cool completely. *Makes 2 loaves.*

## BUTTERSCOTCH FILLING
In small saucepan, combine ½ cup brown sugar, firmly packed, 2 tablespoons butter or margarine, ½ teaspoon cinnamon and ¼ teaspoon salt. Cook over low heat, stirring constantly, until thick and smooth. Cool slightly.

# DOUBLE-GOOD YEAST ROLLS

1 envelope active dry yeast
1⅓ cups very warm water
½ cup vegetable shortening
½ cup sugar
1 teaspoon salt
about 4 cups flour
½ cup butter or margarine,
    melted
Cinnamon Butter (below)
½ cup chopped nuts
½ cup raisins

1. In small bowl, dissolve yeast in very warm water. (Very warm water feels comfortably warm when dropped on wrist.) Let stand 5 minutes.

2. Using electric mixer at high speed, cream vegetable shortening, sugar and salt in large bowl until light and fluffy.

3. Add yeast mixture and 1 cup of the flour. Beat 1 minute, or until mixture is smooth. Stir in enough additional flour to make a soft dough. Turn out onto lightly floured board. Knead 7 to 10 minutes, or until dough is smooth and elastic. Place in greased large bowl. Turn dough to grease all sides. Cover with damp towel. Let rise in warm place free from drafts for 1½ hours, or until doubled in bulk.

4. Punch dough down; divide in half. Knead each half a few times on lightly floured board. Roll out half of dough into a 12 x 17-inch rectangle; cut into 24 circles with a 1½-inch cutter. Melt butter or margarine; divide between two 13 x 9 x 2-inch pans. Set one of the pans aside. Dip both sides of dough circles in the melted butter in the other pan; fold almost in half. Place circles in even rows, almost touching, in the pan.

5. Prepare Cinnamon Butter. Roll remaining dough into a 12 x 17-inch rectangle, ¼ inch thick. Spread cooled Cinnamon Butter evenly over dough. Sprinkle with chopped nuts and raisins. Roll up jelly-roll fashion, starting from long side. Cut into ¾-inch-thick slices. Place cut side down in the second prepared pan. Cover both pans and let rise 1 hour, or until doubled in bulk. Ten minutes before rising time is over, preheat oven to 375° F.

6. Bake rolls and cinnamon buns 15 minutes, or until golden. Immediately turn out cinnamon buns onto heavy-duty aluminum foil. *Makes about 2 dozen rolls and 2 dozen cinnamon buns.*

### CINNAMON BUTTER
In small saucepan, combine ¼ cup butter or margarine, 1 cup light brown sugar, firmly packed, ½ teaspoon cinnamon and ¼ teaspoon salt. Cook over low heat, stirring constantly, until smooth and creamy; cool before using.

## ACORN SQUASH BAKE

2 acorn squash, halved
2 tablespoons butter or
  margarine
2 tablespoons apricot jam
2 tablespoons orange
  liqueur or orange juice

1. Place squash halves cut side up on cookie sheet. Fill centers with butter or margarine, jam and orange liqueur or juice. Cover lightly with aluminum foil.

2. Bake at 325° F for about 50 minutes, or until tender. *Serves 4.*

## BROCCOLI CHEESE BAKE

one 10-ounce package
  frozen chopped broccoli,
  thawed
½ cup process cheese
  spread
½ cup mayonnaise or salad
  dressing
2 tablespoons sesame
  seeds

1. Place thawed chopped broccoli in greased 1-quart glass baking dish.

2. In 1-cup measure, combine cheese spread with mayonnaise or salad dressing. Pour over broccoli and toss to coat evenly. Sprinkle sesame seeds on top.

3. Cover and bake at 325° F for 45 minutes, or until cheese sauce is hot and bubbly, and broccoli is just tender when pierced with a fork. *Serves 4.*

## APPLE CHEESE TARTS

**PASTRY CRUST**
1 cup flour
1 cup grated Cheddar
  cheese
½ teaspoon salt
½ cup butter or margarine
2 tablespoons ice water

**FILLING**
4 large cooking apples,
  peeled and thinly sliced
½ cup sugar
2 tablespoons lemon juice
2 tablespoons whole wheat
  flour
½ teaspoon cinnamon
½ teaspoon nutmeg
pinch of salt

1. Make pastry crust: In small bowl, combine flour, Cheddar cheese and ½ teaspoon salt. Cut in butter or margarine until consistency of cornmeal. Sprinkle ice water over, 1 tablespoon at a time, mixing lightly with a fork until dough forms ball that leaves sides of bowl.

2. Roll out dough to ¼-inch thickness on lightly floured board. Cut 8 circles to fit 2½- to 3-inch muffin pans. Gently press into pans. Cut another 8 circles ¼ inch smaller than top of each tart; set aside. Preheat oven to 425° F.

3. Make filling: In large bowl, combine apples, sugar, lemon juice, whole wheat flour, cinnamon, nutmeg and pinch of salt until well blended. Fill unbaked tart shells. Top with smaller pastry circles.

4. Bake 10 minutes. Reduce heat to 375° F. Bake 30 minutes longer, or until pastry is golden brown. Cool in pans on a wire rack 1 minute. Gently loosen around edges with a long sharp knife; remove to rack. Serve warm or cooled. *Serves 8.*

# COOK-AHEAD DAY FOUR

| | TO COOK | TO STORE AND SERVE |
|---|---|---|
| **I**   **Frozen Lemon Soufflé** <br> **New England Cheesecake** | Prepare Frozen Lemon Soufflé and New England Cheesecake; each one takes 15 to 20 minutes. Freeze soufflé about 6 hours before serving; chill cheesecake several hours before serving. | Freeze soufflé until firm, then overwrap with heavy-duty foil; label and freeze up to 3 months. Let the cheesecake set, then overwrap with heavy-duty foil; store in refrigerator up to 1 week. <br>      Soften soufflé for 5 minutes at room temperature before serving. |
| **II**   **Tuna Casserole** <br> **Tropical Ham Casserole** <br> **Round Steak Casserole** <br> **Chicken and Ham Bake** | Prepare four main dishes for baking. Prepare one at a time (15 to 20 minutes), refrigerating each one on completion. Turn on oven to 350° F. Place Tuna Casserole and Tropical Ham Casserole on bottom shelf of oven; place Round Steak Casserole and Chicken and Ham Bake on the top shelf. Halfway through cooking time, move bottom casseroles to top shelf, top casseroles to bottom shelf. All require about 35 minutes to bake. | Cool to room temperature; tightly cover tops of casseroles with heavy-duty aluminum foil. Label and freeze round steak up to 6 months, all the others up to 3 months. <br>      Thaw casseroles overnight in refrigerator. Heat covered at 350° F for 12 minutes or until hot. |
| **III**   **Chicken Cordon Bleu** <br> **Shrimp Egg Rolls** | Prepare Chicken Cordon Bleu for sautéeing (15 minutes); refrigerate for 1 hour to firm coating. Prepare and cook Shrimp Egg Rolls (1 hour). Sauté the chicken; this takes about 20 to 30 minutes, as it must be done in two batches. | Cool to room temperature. Place in plastic or foil freezer containers; cover tightly with plastic lids or heavy-duty foil. Label and freeze up to 3 months. <br>      Thaw in refrigerator overnight. Place in lightly greased 13 x 9 x 2-inch baking dish. Heat chicken uncovered at 375° F for 20 minutes or until hot; heat egg rolls uncovered at 375° F for 12 minutes or until hot. |

| | TO COOK | TO STORE AND SERVE |
|---|---|---|
| **IV  Crab Quiche**<br>**Pumpkin**<br>**Marmalade Pie** | Preheat oven to 425° F. Prepare Crabmeat Quiche and Pumpkin Marmalade Pie (15 minutes for each). Place the two quiches on bottom shelf of oven and pie on top shelf. Bake for 15 minutes; reduce heat to 350° F. Bake quiches 20 to 30 minutes longer and pie, 50 minutes longer. | Cool to room temperature. Overwrap in heavy-duty foil. Label and freeze up to 3 months.<br>    Thaw quiches in refrigerator overnight. Heat uncovered at 350° F for 10 to 15 minutes or until hot; do not store further. Thaw pie at room temperature. Heat uncovered at 350° F for 12 minutes or just until warm. |

## FROZEN LEMON SOUFFLE

**7 eggs, separated**
**1½ cups sugar**
**2 teaspoons grated lemon**
    **rind**
**⅛ teaspoon salt**
**1½ envelopes unflavored**
    **gelatin**
**¼ cup cold water**
**2¼ cups heavy cream**
**1 slice lemon**
**mint leaves**

1.  First, prepare a collar for a 1½-quart soufflé dish: Cut a 24-inch length of 12-inch-wide waxed paper or aluminum foil; fold in half lengthwise. Wrap around dish so collar stands at least 3 inches above rim; fasten with tape.

2.  In the top of a double boiler over simmering water, beat egg yolks until light and fluffy. Gradually beat in ¾ cup of the sugar. Beat in lemon rind and salt. Stir over low heat until mixture begins to thicken.

3.  Meanwhile, soften gelatin in cold water; stir into egg yolk mixture. Continue stirring until gelatin is dissolved and mixture thickened. Remove from simmering water and cool.

4.  Beat egg whites until frothy. Gradually add the remaining ¾ cup sugar; beat until stiff peaks form. Beat heavy cream until stiff.

5.  Fold meringue, then beaten heavy cream into cooled egg yolk mixture. Pour into prepared soufflé dish and freeze until firm, about 6 hours.

6.  When ready to serve, carefully pull away collar. Garnish center with a twisted lemon slice and a few mint leaves. If desired, pipe a little extra whipped cream in garland around edge. *Serves 8 to 10.*

## NEW ENGLAND CHEESECAKE

6 egg yolks
1 cup sugar
¼ teaspoon salt
2 envelopes unflavored
 gelatin
⅓ cup cold water
four 3-ounce packages
 cream cheese, softened
4 teaspoons vanilla extract
2 cups heavy cream
¾ cup graham cracker
 crumbs

1. In top of double boiler over simmering water, beat egg yolks until fluffy. Beat in sugar and salt. Cook, stirring constantly, until egg yolks begin to thicken.

2. Soften gelatin in cold water; stir into egg yolk mixture. Continue to cook and stir until gelatin is dissolved.

3. Stir in cream cheese and vanilla extract. When thoroughly blended, remove from heat and cool.

4. Beat heavy cream until stiff; fold into cooled cream cheese mixture. Sprinkle graham cracker crumbs evenly over bottom of an oblong 13 x 9 x 2-inch baking pan. Carefully pour cheesecake mixture into pan, trying not to disturb the crumb layer. Chill several hours or overnight. *Serves 12.*

## TUNA CASSEROLE

one 8-ounce package egg
 noodles
boiling water
one 13-ounce can tuna in
 water, drained
one 10¾-ounce can
 condensed cream of
 celery soup
½ cup milk
one 10-ounce package
 frozen peas
2 tablespoons chopped
 onion
2 tablespoons chopped
 parsley
½ teaspoon salt
½ cup packaged cornbread
 stuffing mix

1. Cook noodles in boiling water according to label directions; drain.

2. In greased 2-quart casserole, toss cooked noodles, tuna, condensed celery soup, milk, peas, onion, parsley and salt until well mixed. Top with stuffing mix.

3. Bake at 350° F for 35 minutes, or until stuffing is golden and tuna is bubbly hot. *Serves 4.*

## TROPICAL HAM CASSEROLE

3 cups cooked rice
one 16-ounce can pineapple
    slices in natural juice
2 cups ground cooked ham
8 slices Swiss cheese
1 cup grated coconut

1. Line bottom of a lightly greased 2-quart casserole with cooked rice.

2. Drain pineapple slices, reserving ½ cup of juice. Place pineapple on rice. Top with ham, then cheese; sprinkle with coconut. Pour reserved pineapple juice over all.

3. Bake at 350° F for 30 to 35 minutes, or until bubbly hot. *Serves 4 to 6.*

## ROUND STEAK CASSEROLE

1½ pounds chopped round
    steak
½ cup chopped onion
2 tablespoons vegetable oil
1½ cups cooked rice
one 10-ounce package
    frozen peas
1 cup sliced mushrooms
1 cup tomato juice
2 eggs, slightly beaten
1 teaspoon salt
1 teaspoon crumbled basil
½ teaspoon freshly ground
    pepper

1. In large heavy skillet over moderately high heat, sauté chopped round steak and onion in oil until brown. Place in greased large casserole.

2. Add cooked rice, peas, mushrooms, tomato juice, beaten eggs, salt, basil and pepper. Toss to mix.

3. Bake at 350° F for 35 minutes, or until bubbly hot. *Serves 4 to 6.*

## CHICKEN AND HAM BAKE

6 large chicken breast
    halves, boned
½ cup butter or margarine
1 cup thinly sliced onion
1 cup thinly sliced
    mushrooms
½ pound thinly sliced
    cooked ham
2 tablespoons flour
1 cup chicken broth
½ cup dry white wine

1. In large skillet over moderate heat, sauté chicken breasts in 4 tablespoons of the butter or margarine until browned, about 10 minutes. Remove from skillet. Add 2 tablespoons of the remaining butter or margarine to drippings in skillet. Sauté onion and mushrooms for 5 minutes.

2. Line bottom of a greased 13 x 9 x 2-inch casserole with ham slices. Place chicken over ham. Top with vegetables.

3. Melt remaining 2 tablespoons butter or margarine in the skillet. Add flour and mix until smooth. Add chicken broth. Cook, stirring constantly, until mixture thickens and bubbles, about 3 minutes. Stir in wine. Pour over chicken and vegetables in casserole; cover tightly with aluminum foil.

4. Bake at 350° F for 35 minutes, or until bubbly hot. *Serves 6.*

## CHICKEN CORDON BLEU

8 chicken breast halves,
  skinned and boned
2 teaspoons salt
2 teaspoons pepper
2 teaspoons crumbled basil
2 teaspoons crumbled
  tarragon
½ pound Gruyère cheese, in
  one piece
½ pound cooked ham, in
  one piece
½ cup milk
1 teaspoon salt
¼ teaspoon pepper
1 cup cornflake crumbs
¼ cup butter or margarine

1. Flatten each piece of chicken between two pieces of waxed paper, using wooden mallet. Sprinkle each piece with ¼ teaspoon each salt, pepper, basil and tarragon.

2. Cut both the cheese and the ham into 8 thick strips. Place a cheese and a ham strip at one end of each chicken breast; roll up jelly-roll fashion.

3. In flat plate, mix milk, 1 teaspoon salt and ¼ teaspoon pepper. Place cornflake crumbs on waxed paper. Dip chicken bundles into milk, then roll in cornflake crumbs to coat completely. Secure with toothpicks. Refrigerate 1 hour, to firm up coating and chill the cheese.

4. Melt butter or margarine in large heavy skillet over moderate heat. Sauté chicken on all sides until golden brown and cooked throughout. *Serves 8.*

## SHRIMP EGG ROLLS

**EGG ROLL CREPES**
2 cups water
1½ cups flour
2 eggs
½ teaspoon salt
vegetable oil

**SHRIMP FILLING**
½ pound bacon slices,
  quartered
½ pound shrimp, shelled,
  deveined and chopped
½ cup chopped onion, or
  3 green onions, chopped
2 cups thinly sliced cabbage
one 5-ounce can water
  chestnuts, drained and
  chopped
½ cup sliced mushrooms
1 tablespoon soy sauce

vegetable oil for deep-fat
  frying
hot mustard sauce

1. Make egg roll crêpes: In medium bowl, combine water, flour, eggs and salt until well blended. Let batter stand 15 minutes. Lightly grease a 7-inch crêpe pan with vegetable oil. Heat over moderate heat until oil is bubbly hot. Pour ¼ cup batter into pan. Immediately rotate pan until batter covers bottom. Cook until light brown; turn and cook on other side. Remove to a plate. Continue with remaining batter, stacking crêpes as they are cooked.

2. Make shrimp filling: In wok or large skillet over moderate heat, fry bacon until crisp. Remove with slotted spoon to paper towels. Add shrimp and onion or green onions to drippings in wok. Sauté 1 minute. Add cabbage, water chestnuts, mushrooms and soy sauce. Stir-fry 5 minutes, or until vegetables are tender and shrimp, pink.

3. Place 1 to 2 tablespoons of the shrimp filling on half of each crêpe. Fold sides in and roll up jelly-roll fashion. Secure with toothpicks.

4. In a large heavy saucepan, pour in vegetable oil to a depth of 1½ inches. Heat until temperature reads 375° F on a deep-fat thermometer. Fry egg rolls in fat, a few at a time, until brown and crisp. Drain on paper towels and keep warm until all are cooked. Serve immediately with hot mustard sauce. *Makes about 15 egg rolls.*

## CRAB QUICHE

one 9- to 11-ounce package
   piecrust mix
two 6½-ounce cans
   crabmeat
2 cups grated Gruyère
   cheese
6 eggs, beaten
3 cups light cream
½ cup dry white wine
2 teaspoons salt
¾ teaspoon mace
½ teaspoon white pepper

1. Prepare piecrust mix according to label directions. Roll out to line two 9-inch pie plates. Trim and flute edges of pastry.

2. Preheat oven to 425° F. Drain crab and remove cartilage. Flake, then toss with grated cheese. Divide mixture evenly between pie shells.

3. In medium bowl, combine beaten eggs, light cream, wine, salt, mace and white pepper until smooth. Pour over crab and cheese.

4. Bake 15 minutes. Reduce heat to 350° F. Bake 20 to 30 minutes longer, or until knife inserted 1 inch from edge comes out clean. Let stand 10 minutes before cutting into wedges. *Serves 12.*

## PUMPKIN MARMALADE PIE

one 9- to 11-ounce package
   piecrust mix
one 29-ounce can solid-
   pack pumpkin
1 cup sugar
1 cup brown sugar, firmly
   packed
4 eggs, separated
1 cup light cream
2 teaspoons ground ginger
2 teaspoons ground
   cinnamon
¼ teaspoon ground cloves
¼ teaspoon ground nutmeg
1 teaspoon salt
½ cup orange marmalade
ginger-flavored whipped
   cream (optional)

1. Prepare piecrust mix according to label directions. Divide in half; wrap and refrigerate half for another use. Roll out remaining half to line a 10-inch pie plate. Trim and flute edge of pastry.

2. Preheat oven to 425° F. In large bowl, combine pumpkin with sugar and brown sugar. Stir in egg yolks, light cream, ginger, cinnamon, cloves, nutmeg and salt until smooth. Fold in marmalade.

3. Beat egg whites slightly in medium bowl; brush pie shell with egg whites. Continue beating remaining egg whites. Fold into pumpkin mixture.

4. Pour pumpkin mixture into pie shell. Bake 15 minutes. Reduce heat to 350° F; bake 50 minutes longer, or until knife inserted in center comes out clean. Serve with ginger-flavored whipped cream, if you wish. *Serves 8.*

# COOK-AHEAD DAY FIVE

| | | TO COOK | TO STORE AND SERVE |
|---|---|---|---|
| I | **Pork Chop and Potato Casserole Chocolate Chess Pie** | Make Pork Chop and Potato Casserole (20 minutes to prepare and up to 1½ hours to bake at 325° F). Make Chocolate Chess Pie (15 minutes to prepare and 40 minutes to bake at 325° F). | Cool to room temperature. Tightly cover top of casserole with heavy-duty foil; overwrap pie with heavy-duty foil. Label and freeze pie up to 6 months, casserole up to 3 months. Thaw casserole in refrigerator overnight; heat covered at 325° F for 25 minutes or until hot. Thaw pie at room temperature; heat uncovered at 325° F for 12 minutes or just until warm. |
| II | **Coconut Pound Cake Mini Mushroom Meat Loaves with Bake-Along Rice** | Increase oven temperature to 350° F. Prepare Coconut Pound Cake (15 minutes); bake on bottom shelf of oven for 1½ hours. (Allow 10 additional minutes to glaze cake after baking.) Prepare Mini Mushroom Meat Loaves and Bake-Along Rice (a total of 15 minutes preparation time). Bake side by side on top shelf of oven for 45 minutes, adding Japanese-style vegetables after 35 minutes. | Cool to room temperature. Overwrap pound cake in heavy-duty foil; tightly cover top of meat loaves and rice with foil. Label and freeze up to 6 months. Thaw pound cake at room temperature; the cake may be sliced and toasted, if desired. Thaw meat loaves and rice in refrigerator overnight; heat covered at 350° F for 10 minutes or until hot. |
| III | **Roast Beef and Potato Bubble Sherried Green Beans** | Prepare Roast Beef and Potato Bubble and Sherried Green Beans; allow about 15 minutes for each. The roast beef simmers for about 20 minutes, and the green beans, about 15 minutes. | Cool to room temperature. Spoon roast beef into plastic freezer containers, leaving ½- to ¾-inch headroom. (Mixture will expand on freezing.) Cover tightly with plastic lids. Spoon green beans into plastic freezer container; cover tightly with plastic lid. Label and freeze both dishes up to 3 months. Thaw beef overnight in refrigerator; heat covered |

| | TO COOK | TO STORE AND SERVE |
|---|---|---|
| | | over medium heat until piping hot. Serve over biscuits as directed. Thaw beans at room temperature for 30 minutes; heat covered over low heat to thaw completely; heat until hot. |
| **IV Stuffed Chicken Breasts McCoy**<br>**Easy Chicken Breasts**<br>**Eggplant Casserole**<br>**Bourbon Peaches** | Maintain oven temperature at 350° F. Prepare Stuffed Chicken Breasts McCoy (30 minutes); bake on bottom shelf of oven for 45 minutes. (Allow 15 additional minutes to make a sauce after baking.) Prepare Easy Chicken Breasts (10 minutes) and bake on top shelf for 45 minutes. Prepare Eggplant Casserole (20 minutes) and bake on bottom shelf for 20 minutes. Prepare Bourbon Peaches (5 minutes) and bake on top shelf for about 10 minutes. | Cool to room temperature. Place Stuffed Chicken Breasts McCoy in 13 x 9 x 2-inch baking dish. Tightly cover baking dishes with heavy-duty foil. Label and freeze peaches up to 6 months, all other dishes up to 3 months.<br>Thaw overnight in refrigerator (peaches can be thawed at room temperature). Heat chicken dishes covered at 350° F for 20 minutes. Heat Eggplant Casserole covered at 350° F for 10 to 15 minutes. Bourbon Peaches can be served cold or heated covered at 350° F for 5 minutes. |

# PORK CHOP AND POTATO CASSEROLE

**4 center-cut pork chops**
**2 tablespoons vegetable oil**
**one 10¾-ounce can condensed cream of celery soup**
**⅓ cup water**
**4 cups sliced peeled potatoes**
**salt and pepper to taste**
**1 cup thinly sliced onion**
**1 teaspoon crumbled basil**

1. In a large skillet over moderately high heat, brown pork chops, two at a time, in hot oil; brown 5 minutes per side.

2. In small bowl, combine condensed celery soup and water. Spoon half into greased 1½-quart casserole.

3. Add half of the potatoes in an even layer; sprinkle with salt and pepper. Top with half of the onions. Repeat layering with remaining soup, potatoes and onions. Top with browned pork chops. Sprinkle with basil.

4. Bake at 325° F for 1 to 1½ hours, or until chops and potatoes are tender when pierced with a fork. *Serves 4.*

## CHOCOLATE CHESS PIE

one 9- to 11-ounce package
  piecrust mix
⅓ cup butter or margarine
two 1-ounce squares
  unsweetened chocolate
5 eggs
1¾ cups sugar
2 tablespoons whole wheat
  flour
½ teaspoon salt
½ cup unflavored yogurt

1. Preheat oven to 325° F. Prepare piecrust mix according to label directions. Divide in half; wrap and refrigerate half for another use. Roll out remaining half to line a 10-inch pie plate. Trim and flute edge of pastry.

2. In small saucepan over very low heat, melt butter or margarine with chocolate. Cool slightly.

3. Using electric mixer at high speed, beat eggs in medium bowl until thick and lemon colored. Gradually add sugar and beat until well blended. Beat in flour and salt. Beat in chocolate mixture and the yogurt. Pour into pie shell.

4. Bake 40 minutes, or until puffy and golden. Do not overbake. (Filling will settle and thicken.) Cool pie to room temperature before serving. *Serves 8.*

## COCONUT POUND CAKE

1½ cups butter or
  margarine, softened
3 cups sugar
5 eggs
⅔ cup evaporated milk
5 cups sifted flour
1 teaspoon vanilla extract
1 teaspoon almond extract
one 8-ounce package
  sweetened shredded
  coconut

**GLAZE**
1 cup sugar
½ cup water
1 teaspoon coconut extract

1. Preheat oven to 350° F. Cream butter or margarine in large bowl of electric mixer. Gradually add the 3 cups of sugar, beating until fluffy.

2. Add eggs, one at a time, beating well after each addition. Pour evaporated milk into a 1-cup measure; add enough water to make 1 cup liquid. Alternately add the flour and the milk to the egg mixture, beating well after each addition.

3. Add vanilla and almond extracts. Fold in the shredded coconut; pour batter into a well-greased and floured 10-inch bundt pan. Bake 1½ hours, or until cake begins to pull away from sides of pan. Cool cake in pan on rack for about 35 to 40 minutes, then turn out on rack and complete cooling.

4. Make glaze: In a small saucepan, combine 1 cup sugar and ½ cup water. Boil rapidly for 2 or 3 minutes. Cool; stir in coconut extract. Use a spoon to drizzle glaze over cake. *Serves 10 to 12.*

## MINI MUSHROOM MEAT LOAVES WITH BAKE-ALONG RICE

1 pound lean ground beef,
  round or sirloin
half of ¾-ounce envelope
  onion soup mix
1 cup fresh bread cubes
¼ cup milk
1 egg
1 teaspoon salt
¼ teaspoon pepper
6 large mushroom caps
Bake-Along Rice (below)
one 10-ounce package
  frozen Japanese-style
  vegetables in sauce,
  slightly thawed

1. Preheat oven to 350° F. In medium bowl, combine ground beef, onion soup mix, bread cubes, milk, egg, salt and pepper just until blended. Form into 6 patties and place in a greased 13 x 9 x 2-inch baking dish. Top with mushroom caps.

2. Prepare Bake-Along Rice. Bake patties and rice for about 35 minutes.

3. Add slightly thawed Japanese-style vegetables to rice. Bake 10 minutes longer, or until rice is tender and patties are cooked. *Serves 4 to 6.*

### BAKE-ALONG RICE
In greased 1½-quart casserole, combine 2¼ cups of water, 1 cup of long-grain rice, and half of ¾-ounce envelope onion soup mix. Cover with aluminum foil. Bake along with Mini Mushroom Meat Loaves.

## ROAST BEEF AND POTATO BUBBLE

2 cups cubed cooked roast
  beef
3 cups cubed peeled
  potatoes
½ cup chopped onion
2 cups leftover beef gravy,
  or 2 cups beef gravy
  (from two 10¾-ounce
  cans)
salt and pepper to taste
2 tablespoons flour
¼ cup water
hot biscuits

1. In medium saucepan, combine beef, potatoes, onion, gravy, and salt and pepper. Bring to boiling point; lower heat. Cover saucepan. Simmer 20 minutes, or until potatoes are tender when pierced with a fork.

2. In a 1-cup measure, stir flour into water until smooth. Add to saucepan. Cook, stirring often, until mixture thickens and bubbles, about 3 minutes. Serve over hot biscuits, accompanied by a bowl of spiced applesauce. *Serves 4.*

## SHERRIED GREEN BEANS

3 slices bacon, chopped
1 pound fresh green beans
1 cup chopped green onions
1 teaspoon salt
½ teaspoon sugar
¼ cup chicken broth
one 5-ounce can water
    chestnuts, drained and
    thinly sliced
1 tablespoon dry sherry

1. In large wok or skillet over moderately high heat, sauté bacon until crisp. Remove with slotted spoon and drain on paper towels.

2. Sauté green beans and green onions in bacon drippings for 3 minutes, or until beans turn bright green. Sprinkle with salt and sugar; pour chicken broth over. Cover wok and lower heat. Simmer 10 minutes, or until beans are barely tender.

3. Stir in water chestnuts and sherry. Cook 1 minute longer, or until vegetables are crisply tender. Sprinkle with chopped bacon. *Serves 4.*

## STUFFED CHICKEN BREASTS McCOY

1½ cups long-grain and wild
    rice mix
2 cups chopped mushrooms
½ cup butter or margarine
4 whole chicken breasts,
    skinned and boned
⅓ cup liver pâté
2 cups chicken broth
1 cup dry white wine
2 cups seedless green
    grapes, halved

1. Prepare rice according to label directions. In small skillet, sauté mushrooms in half of the butter or margarine until soft; add to cooked rice, stirring gently to mix well.

2. Preheat oven to 350° F. Spread insides of chicken breasts with pâté, then fill with rice-mushroom mixture. Roll up or fold over to enclose filling. Secure with toothpicks. Place stuffed chicken breasts in greased shallow baking dish. Dot with remaining butter or margarine.

3. Bake for 45 minutes, or until chicken is tender; remove chicken to a heated serving platter and keep warm.

4. Deglaze baking dish with chicken broth and wine, simmering over medium heat for 10 minutes. Add grapes and simmer 2 minutes longer, or until grapes are heated through. Pour sauce over chicken. *Serves 4.*

# EASY CHICKEN BREASTS

4 chicken breasts, halved
4 slices bacon, halved
2 cups sliced mushrooms
one 11-ounce can artichoke
  hearts, drained and
  quartered
1 cup finely chopped onion
1 cup dry white wine
1 teaspoon crumbled
  oregano
1 teaspoon salt

1. Preheat oven to 350° F.

2. Place chicken breasts skin side up in large heatproof baking dish. Top each half of a chicken breast with half of a bacon slice. Sprinkle mushrooms, artichoke hearts, onion, wine, oregano and salt over chicken and bacon.

3. Bake for 45 minutes, or until chicken is tender and bacon is cooked. *Serves 4.*

# EGGPLANT CASSEROLE          02/10/08

one 29-ounce can whole
  tomatoes
2 bay leaves
3 cups diced peeled
  eggplant
1 cup chopped onion
1 cup chopped celery
½ cup chopped parsley
¼ cup olive oil
½ cup dry seasoned bread
  crumbs
¼ cup grated Parmesan
  cheese
2 tablespoons butter or
  margarine

1. Preheat oven to 350° F. In a medium saucepan, simmer tomatoes (and their liquid) and bay leaves until thickened and reduced to 2 cups of sauce. Remove bay leaves.

2. In a large skillet, sauté eggplant, onion, celery and parsley in olive oil until soft.

3. Mix the reduced tomato sauce and the sautéed vegetables in a 1½-quart casserole. Top with bread crumbs and Parmesan cheese. Dot with butter or margarine.

4. Bake 20 minutes, or until topping is golden and vegetables and sauce are bubbly hot. *Serves 6.*

Takes a long time to reduce tomatoes

# BOURBON PEACHES

one 30-ounce can large
  peach halves, drained
6 to 8 almond macaroons,
  crushed
2 tablespoons bourbon
1 cup heavy cream, stiffly
  beaten

1. Preheat oven to 350° F.

2. Place peach halves hollow side up in heatproof dish. Combine crushed macaroons with bourbon; fill peach halves.

3. Bake 10 minutes, or until macaroon mixture is golden and bubbly. Serve hot or cold with stiffly beaten heavy cream. *Serves 4.*

# INDEX

Acorn squash bake, 121
Apples:
  baked, 69
  cheese tarts, 121
  foam, 71
  in snow, 76
Artichoke bottoms with caviar, 64
Asparagus and beef stir-fry, 33, **51**

Banana coffee cake, 105
Bananas, baked, 84
Bean and beef burgers, 13
Beans:
  green, in lemon sauce, 81
  green, sherried, 132
  knockwurst and, 16
  navy, soup, 108
Beef:
  and bean oriental, 11
  chili con carne, 12
  corned, Belgian, 14
  gumbo Joes, 11
  pot pie, 103
  roast, and potato bubble, 131
  stew, orientale, 116
  stir-fry, with asparagus, 33, **51**
  see also Hamburger; Meat
    loaves; Steak
Belgian corned beef, 14
Blintz sandwiches, quick, 28
Blueberry Betty, 78
Bluefish:
  creamy piquant, 48
  in-and-out, 95
Bluefish menu, work plan, 94
Bread:
  two-for-one, 119
  yeast rolls, double-good, 120
Broccoli:
  cheese bake, 121
  scallop and, stir-fry, 23
Brussels sprouts, smoked pork
    chops and, 15

Cabbage rolls, ham-stuffed, 118
Casseroles:
  chili-cheese, 12
  crab, creamy, 53
  crisp and savory, 17

Casseroles (continued)
  eggplant, 133
  fish and spinach, 48
  ham, tropical, 125
  pork chop and potato, 129
  round steak, 125
  shell macaroni, 112
  shrimp, sweet-and-sour, 103
  spinach-tomato, 60
  squash, 102
  tuna, 124
  tuna noodle, 55
Cheese:
  Brie en croute, 83
  broccoli bake, 121
  chili-, casserole, 12
  dogs with bacon, 43
  franks, quick, 17
  hamburger and, with noodles,
    37
  -hamwiches, 16
  rarebits, 27
  shrimp bake, 96
  -steak sandwiches, 35
  wine-, toast, 27
Cheesecake, New England, 124
Cheese pie, creamy chocolate,
    113
Cherries jubilee, 65
Chicken:
  breasts, easy, 133
  breasts, Italian, 19
  breasts, stuffed, McCoy, 132
  Chinese, 117
  cordon bleu, 126
  curry, 117
  delight, Japanese, 19
  and ham bake, 125
  -noodle dinner, sausage and, 16
  roll puffs, 20
  sandwiches, guacamole, 21
  sauté, Italian, 43
  shrimp-, mountain, 98
  stir-fry, almond, 44
Chicken livers:
  with mushrooms, 45
  on rice, 44
  stroganoff, 20
  veal scallops with, 77

Chili:
  baked, 111
  -cheese casserole, 12
  con carne, tangy, 12
  quick quick, 38
Chocolate chess pie, 130
Clam fritters, 23
Coconut pound cake, 130
Coffee cake, banana, 105
Coffee mousse, 90
Corn:
  pudding, quick, 89
  and tomato chowder, 30
Corned beef, Belgian, 14
Coulibiac, 91
Coulibiac menu, work plan, **88,**
    90
Crab:
  casserole, creamy, 53
  double quick, 53
  Mornay, easy, 25
  mushrooms stuffed with, 73
  quiche, 127
Cucumber and peas, 93
Cupcakes, black and white, 105

Eggplant casserole, 133
Egg rolls, shrimp, 126
Eggs:
  Benedict, 55
  corned beef hash and, 35
  Gruyère, 26
  roast beef hash and, 12
Escargots in mushroom caps, 80

Fettuccine Alfredo, 30
Fettuccine verde, 63
Filet mignon menu, work plan,
    62, **85**
Fish:
  baked, 48
  casserole, with spinach, 47
  in dill sauce, 47
  seafood roll-ups, easy, 25
  soup, Norwegian, 21
  see also specific seafood
Fish sticks with sour cream
    dressing, 22
Flank steak menu, work plan, 67

Frankfurters:
   cheese, with bacon, 43
   cheese, quick, 17
Fudge tarts, 104

Grapefruit, minted, 97
Green beans, *see* Beans
Griottes, 83
Griottes menu, work plan, 83
Gumbo Joes, 11

Ham:
   -asparagus Mornay, 71
   and biscuit loaf, 15
   cabbage rolls stuffed with, 118
   casserole, tropical, 125
   and chicken bake, 125
   grilled, with peach sauce, 15
   loaf, baked, 112
   with pineapple and apricots, 42,
     **52**
   and spinach crescents, 42
   waffles, 42
Ham-asparagus menu, work plan,
   71
Hamburger:
   bean and beef burgers, 13
   and cheese with noodles, 37
   soup, 38
   steak, in wine sauce, 10
   stroganoff, 36
Hash and eggs, 12, 35

Ice cream, vanilla, with apricot
   sauce, 72
Italian chicken breasts, 19
Italian pasta potpourri, 29, **50**

Japanese chicken delight, 19

Knockwurst and beans, 16

Lamb, skewered, 80
Lamb chop menu, work plan, 78
Lasagne, skillet, 37
Lentil soup, 102
Lobster Newburg, 24

Macaroni:
   green and gold, 28
   "plus" salad, 28
   shell, casserole, 112
   *see also* Pasta

Manicotti Parmesan, 58
Marzipan tarts, 113
Meatballs, Scandinavian, 70
Meat loaves:
   mini mushroom, with bake-
     along rice, 131
   my mother's, 36
Mousse, coffee, 90
Mushrooms:
   chicken livers with, 45
   crab-stuffed, 73
   escargots stuffed in, 80
   stuffed, 62

Norwegian fish soup, 21

Pancake flambé, puff, 81
Pasta:
   fettuccine Alfredo, 30
   fettuccine verde, 63
   Italian pasta potpourri, 29, **50**
   lasagne, skillet, 37
   manicotti Parmesan, 58
   pepperoni pasta, 29
   *see also* Macaroni
Peaches, Bourbon, 133
Pear Betty, 89
Peas, cucumber and, 93
Pepperoni:
   pasta, 29
   -vegetable pot, 18
Pepper steak, 34
Pies:
   beef pot, 103
   chocolate chess, 130
   creamy chocolate cheese, 113
   pumpkin marmalade, 127
   shepherds', 35
   spinach, 72
Pineapple, strawberries and,
   Chantilly, 66
Pita bread, stuffed, 30
Pizza, make-your-own, 57
Pork chops:
   lemon, 41
   with oregano, 41
   and potato casserole, 129
   smoked, and Brussels sprouts,
     15
   Veronika, 82
Pork chop menu, work plan, 82
Pork tenderloin Guatemala, 89

Pork tenderloin menu, work plan,
   89
Potatoes au gratin, 95
Potato soup, Pennsylvania
   creamy, 109
Pound cake, coconut, 130
Pumpkin marmalade pie, 127

Quiche:
   crab, 127
   Mr. Robertson's, 57
   yogurt, 26

Rarebit:
   with mushrooms, Welsh, 27, **49**
   on toast, 27
Rice:
   bake-along, 131
   medley, 102
   risotto, 75
   tuna on, 54
Risotto, 75
Roast beef:
   hash and eggs, 12
   and potato bubble, 131
Rolls, yeast, double-good, 120
Roll-ups:
   crusty meat and vegetable, 18
   seafood, easy, 25
   turkey, 45

Salad:
   curried turkey, 46
   macaroni "plus," 28
   tuna, on a roll, 54
Salmon:
   Coulibiac, 91
   croquettes, quick, 22
   soufflé, 92
Salmon soufflé menu, work plan, 92
Sandwiches:
   blintz, quick, 28
   cheese-hamwiches, 16
   cheese-steak, 35
   guacamole chicken, 21
   Reuben, easy, 14
   tuna, Madras, 26
   turkey, open-face hot, 46
   veal, favorite, 41
Sauces:
   lemon, 93
   Ti-Malise, 84

Sauerbraten, thirty-minute, 10
Sausage:
    and chicken-noodle dinner, 16
    in mushroom sauce, 116
Scallop and broccoli stir-fry, 23
Scampi, 97
Scampi menu, work plan, 97
Scandinavian meatballs, 70
Scandinavian meatballs menu,
        work plan, 69
Shepherds' pie, 35
Shrimp:
    casserole, sweet-and-sour, 103
    cheese bake, 96
    -chicken mountain, 98
    with Chinese vegetables, 24
    egg rolls, 126
    scampi, 97
Shrimp cheese menu, work plan,
        96
Shrimp-chicken menu, work plan,
        98
Sirloin steak menu, work plan, 66
Skewered lamb menu, work plan,
        80
Soufflé:
    carrot, 110
    lemon, frozen, 123
    lemon, warm, 61
    raspberry, 68
    salmon, 92
Soup:
    chestnut, 82
    corn and tomato chowder, 30
    double vegetable bisque, 108
    fish, Norwegian, 21
    hamburger, 38
    lentil, 102
    navy bean, 108
    Pennsylvania creamy potato,
        109
    turkey, 101
    yogurt, cold, 94

Soup-er supper, 17
Spinach:
    crescents, with ham, 42
    fish and, casserole, 48
    pie, 72
    -tomato casserole, 60
    tomatoes stuffed with, 67
Squash:
    acorn, bake, 121
    casserole, 102
    country club, 58
Steak:
    au poivre, 61
    with black butter, 32
    budget, stew, 34
    -cheese sandwiches, 35
    cube, Béarnaise, 32
    cube, with Cognac sauce, 32
    Dianne, 65
    flank, stuffed, 68
    minute, stuffed, 104
    pepper, 34
    round, casserole, 125
    sukiyaki, 33
Steak au poivre menu, work plan,
        60
Steak Diane menu, work plan, 64
Strawberries and pineapple
        Chantilly, 66
Sukiyaki, 33
Sweet potato puffle, 110


Tamale dish, lazy day, 13
Tarts:
    apple cheese, 121
    fudge, 104
    marzipan, 113
Ti-Malise sauce, 84
Tomatoes:
    casserole, with spinach, 60
    cherry, garlicked, 63
    stuffed with spinach, 67

Tortilla, Pablo's, 56
Tuna:
    casserole, 124
    noodle casserole, 55
    on rice, 54
    salad on a roll, 54
    sandwiches, Madras, 26
    stir-fry, 25
Turkey:
    creamed, 46
    roll-ups, 45
    salad, curried, 46
    sandwiches, open-face hot, 46
    soup, 101
    tasty, 19

Veal:
    champignon, 14
    creamy ground, 40
    paprika, 74
    roulades, skillet, 39
    sandwiches, favorite, 41
    sauté, 73
    scallops, with chicken livers, 77
    zucchini, stuffed with, 40
    in wine, 39
Veal paprika menu, work plan, 74
Veal sauté menu, work plan, 72
Veal scallops menu, work plan, 76
Vegetable compass, 79

Welsh rarebit with mushrooms,
        27, **49**
Wine-cheese toast, 27

Yogurt "quiche," 26
Yogurt soup, cold, 94

Zabaglione over fruit, 75
Zucchini:
    bake, 65
    stuffed with veal, 40